the
NAKED SOLDIER

the
NAKED SOLDIER

A True Story of the
French Foreign Legion

Tony Sloane

First published in 2004 by Vision, a division of Satin Publications Ltd.
101 Southwark Street
London SE1 0JF
UK
info@visionpaperbacks.co.uk
www.visionpaperbacks.co.uk
Publisher: Sheena Dewan

A catalogue record for this book is available from the British Library.

ISBN: 1-904132-60-X

2 4 6 8 10 9 7 5 3 1

Cover photo: © Thomas Hartwell/Time and Life Pictures/Getty Images
Cover and text design by ok?design
Printed and bound in the UK by
Mackays of Chatham Ltd, Chatham, Kent

For all that take the time to listen and understand

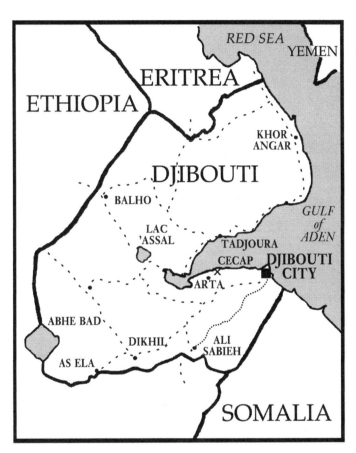

.... CHAPTER 1

The sound of a thousand strange voices produced a small ball of fire in the pit of my stomach. They sang a French translation of a Waffen-SS marching song. It told of war and death, honour and fidelity, of the way of life for the 2nd Parachute Regiment (2eme REP). I stood there in a sea of culture. Hardly more than a boy, I sang with all my might, my lungs straining to compete with the hard, chilling voices of men who would be as happy beating you to death as they would be to go to their own deaths. Maybe I was a little out of my depth.

An order to stand at ease was shouted. *Au repos*: we stood quite still but relaxed. I looked at the stars. The night was clear and warm with a few wisps of cloud covering the moon in a hazy glow. A dozen small green lights circled like vultures: the section parachute reconnaissance swooped towards the parade square like silent giant bats. Their canopies flapped noiselessly in the wind. I thought how I wanted to be like them.

The colonel said a few words, but I couldn't understand them all. Only a few months prior to this *Fête de St Michel*, an annual festival celebrating parachuting troops, I hardly spoke a word of French.

*

At 18 years old, I hitch-hiked from Norwich to Dover, only accepting lifts from people who seemed genuine. A man in his fifties pulled up next to me looking half drunk, trying to talk me into getting in. I wasn't stupid: I knew when I was being coerced, and I didn't even have my thumb out at the time. I was just south of London and tired, so I found a small clear area on the side of the road next to a field of cows where the bushes hid my tent quite well. I slept well: I had grown used to sleeping on the floor since I had been travelling around the UK roaming from job to job, without making plans. I preferred to see what life would throw at me.

I had been bouncing from place to place since the age of three. My parents' divorce had meant a life kindly dictated by the state. I had never spent more than three years in the same place, passing from school to school, collecting friends with sell-by dates. For the past year and a half since I left school I had drifted from various menial jobs – washing dishes, mixing concrete, stacking shelves and farm work. I was now used to setting up home on any street corner, in farmers' fields, camp sites and hostels. I could live comfortably on next to nothing and my only concern was where the next meal or pay cheque was coming from.

Later, as I sat on the bow of the ferry and watched the white cliffs disappear, I realized I didn't know what I was doing. I had a rucksack, a tent, a few clothes and £70 in my pocket and I was off to see what would happen. Looking back it seems to me a brave thing to do. I was young and taking my chances. I had decided to hitch to

Gibraltar and maybe find some labouring work. I felt that life was to be experienced to the full and the world was out there to find that experience.

Shortly after my arrival in France I met Scouse, Dave, John, Frank and Mark. They called me over as I walked from the ferry terminal to Calais town centre.

'Oi mate! ... where ya goin?'

I looked across to the group. I didn't know whether I should go over: I quite enjoyed travelling alone because I was always my own boss. Dave was wearing a dirty white t-shirt, jeans and trainers. I walked over.

'You got a tent?'

'Yeah.'

'Great ... we've only got one tent for five of us.' With that I felt I was committed to staying, so he helped me pitch my tent.

'So where you goin?'

'I don't know ... I was thinking of going to Gibraltar.'

'Nah don't bovver ... Mark knows a farm down south where we can work for the summer ... you coming?'

I agreed to go and we went to the town. I soon discovered that you could travel for free in France if you had a little cunning. We would use the free bus from the ferry terminal to get to town and back to the bit of wasteland in which we were camped. In a small café in Calais I met my first French girl: Annabelle was 17, short with a spotty face and spoke a little English. We spoke for the evening in broken English and French about her studies in college. I wasn't very experienced but I did get her address and we would write to each other for a few years. Dave hooked up with her friend.

But we couldn't stay in Calais for ever. The summer was just beginning. April was a good time to start travelling and working for the summer. We only had one small problem: we were broke and we had no idea how we would get there. Of course it was Scouse who came up with the answer. He was short and deathly skinny with small untrusting eyes, but I felt we could get along for a while. He had been travelling and seemed to have an idea of how to get along by the skin of his teeth.

We would simply get on the train and not pay. At the next stop we would get thrown off. Then we would just get on the next train. So we packed up, said our good-byes to Annabelle and her friend and boarded the train for Paris. Our plan was working. Each time we were asked for a *billet* (ticket) we would just open our palms and in our worst French accents say 'no problem'. The response was not warm. Occasionally, one of the inspectors would just laugh.

'Moi, pas de problème, vous oui problème!' 'Me no problem, you, yes problem!'

Our passport numbers were taken and we were given penalty tickets, which we took to the nearest refuse bin. It was while we were sleeping rough in Lyon train station that the group decided to split. Scouse and I decided that we would hitch to St Tropez via Marseille and have a look around there. That turned out to be one of the deciding factors in my future. The others were going to continue jumping trains.

That morning we tried to hitch. We walked and put our thumbs out, but it took hours to get a lift. The French don't hitch, so they don't pick up. Only French people who had travelled or foreigners to France stopped. We tried for hours to find a decent place to hitch and ended up at a service station. We tried but it was useless.

Hope approached in the form two British women who pulled up to refuel.

'Hi! You English? Where you going?' We had seen the number plate and mistakenly thought our common nationality would help. Surely they would help us fellow countrymen? 'We were looking for a lift.'

'Well, you should have made your arrangements before. You're not getting in with us.' The woman lifted her chin high and turned away to ignore us, so we walked back to our prime spot and sat on the grass.

'This is shit … no one ever picks up two blokes!'

'Not those two stuck up bitches anyway.' It took another couple of days before we finally arrived in Marseille.

Marseille was the underworld of the south of France. Corner shops sold porn and knives. Every possible type of weapon you could imagine from a Hollywood horror could be found in Marseille: knuckle dusters with spikes and a knife protruding from the handle for a punch and stab; extendible metal batons; huge Rambo knives and an array of guns. Down narrow alleys where the sun never reached, seedy characters dressed in leather jackets would deal in anything and everything: counterfeit money for genuine, drugs for guns, watches, stolen bags, passports – you name it you could get it in Marseille. We wandered the streets and drank tea, as Scouse was teetotal, by the port. The buildings were tall and narrow. They were dotted with small dirty square windows where curtains would twitch and faces lurk in the gloom behind them. Every now and then we would be approached.

'Nice watch. Is it expensive?' This was a question directed not through genuine interest but to find if it was worth stealing.

'Could you spare me some change? I am trying to get back to Germany.'

'Do you want some girls? Pretty girls – come, come.'

'Hashish, hashish.'

In Marseille train station, someone a bit different came up to us. His medals glinted in the May sun, the creases on his shirt were sharp and his white hat almost glowed like a t-shirt on a Persil ad. He had heard us speaking English. I didn't ask his name. He told us about his recent trip to Chad in Central Africa. He was on leave from the French Foreign Legion. I was fascinated by his stories and he suggested that we should join.

I had read a book written by Simon Murray a couple of years previously that had got me interested in the Legion. My brother Colin had been in the army since the age of 16, and I had listened to him and been influenced by his stories of travel and adventure. I'd been hill walking with him a few times and watched him train. Wanting to do something different in my life, something special, I thought this fitted quite well with my current situation. I was seeking adventure, travel and experience.

Scouse and I decided to go to St Tropez and earn some money. Unfortunately, I didn't have any skills with which to do so. But Scouse could do one thing really well: he could act like a robot – 'robotics' he called it.

During the day we went to the beach and looked at the girls. We sat in terraced cafés nestled between the tall, stone buildings shadowing narrow cobbled streets. We drank tea and watched the bourgeois French ladies glide past, immaculate with their make up, coordinating clothes and carrying the tiny dogs that symbolise wealth and good upbringing. In the evenings we busked or looked at the people on their huge yachts. They sat on the deck and had waiters serve them champagne. I thought how I would like to live like that for a while. In my jealousy I branded them ignorant of the world. I associated them with the two girls that wouldn't give us a lift. Strange how our opinions are formed – influenced and prejudiced by our previous experiences.

Scouse had a couple of annoying traits that I found hard to deal with. He was about ten years older than me. He reminded me of my father, who also only drank tea.

Dad was a reformed alcoholic and a teetotaller, although I didn't know that much about him. At 14 years old he worked down the Yorkshire coalmines, before becoming a carpenter. Somewhere along the line I believe he was married and had three daughters before meeting my mother. At one point he became a serious meths drinker on the streets.

I on the other hand was keen for a couple of pints and a social chat. But after a couple of weeks in St Tropez I'd had enough. Scouse had this ridiculous idea of travelling all the way back to Liverpool to collect his stereo to improve his robotics act. I could not see the point. I suggested saving a little money and buying one in France. It was time to part company.

I still hadn't forgotten the legionnaire at the train station and had already made the decision to join: I had a philosophy of life that I still retain. I didn't want to grow old and think – what if? What if I had done this or that? What if I had taken the chance? I realize that I could not do all my 'what ifs', but I could try to minimise them.

I naturally asked Scouse if he would join me, but understandably he refused. I had learned from the legionnaire that I should join with no possessions, as the Legion took everything you had from you. I gave Scouse everything except for the rucksack, which we traded in a café in Toulon for a couple of croissants and a pot of tea. The plump, tanned lady owner looked at us as if we were mad, but after a little negotiation she agreed. I wrote a couple of letters; one to my older brother Colin telling him what I was doing and one to my father telling him that I wouldn't be around for a while, as I didn't want him interfering.

I left Scouse sitting outside the café in Toulon and never saw him again. I was on my own and it felt good, stepping forward into another stage of my life. The train from Toulon to Marseille stopped at Aubagne, where the 1er Régiment Etrangère is based. The regiment deals with all the administration and is where you go to join and leave.

I found myself at the gates in the early evening – they were inset with the golden flame of the Legion above which glowed 'Legio Patria Nostra' (the Legion's motto: 'The Legion is our country'). Behind the gates in the shadows stood a legionnaire. He was dressed in a khaki green uniform on which a pair of silver wings glinted upon his right breast. Through the dazzling light of his torch I could just see the sombre outline of his face. His features were hidden under the shadow of his white képi, his lips were tight and his eyes dark beneath thick black eyebrows. To my surprise he spoke to me in a thick, accented English.

'What you want?'

'I have come to join the Foreign Legion.' He grunted to himself and walked into the shadows. Still observing me from the gloom he spoke on his radio and returned into view after a brief conversation in French.

'You must come back … in the morning.'

I immediately wished I had kept my things. I had a few francs left for food but nothing else. I wandered back towards the rail station contemplating my lodgings for the night. As I walked past a local police station I thought, why not? Inside, I tried to explain my situation, but they were not prepared to take me in for the night. Instead they took me into a small room and stripped me of all my clothes and carried out a thorough search. I didn't care: it was one more event that would drive me further into the future. Every setback, every little part of my life that angered me, motivated me.

Back on the streets outside I looked around until I found a convenient space behind a garage that didn't smell too strongly of urine, and where the cardboard boxes were reasonably dry. After a restless night, I woke early in the morning with a tacky mouth, rubbed my eyes and tried to shake the cold from my bones. At the train station I washed my face in sinks in the toilet. I had left my toothbrush and towel (the only items that I didn't leave Scouse) on the side of the road somewhere the previous night. Inside the café I ordered a croissant and coffee. I held the cup tight, savouring the warmth. It was still dark outside and I was tired. I wondered if I was doing the right thing – I could still try something else.

Armed only with my passport and a few centimes, I tried once more at the gates. And this time I was let in and left in another small room to wait.

.... CHAPTER 2

This was probably to give me time to think about the very difficult choice I had made: joining a foreign army when you don't speak the language, you don't know what is going to happen or if you will ever come back, whether for the next five years you will be living in the desert fighting for your life. I picked up a magazine called *Képi Blanc*, which featured every regiment in the Legion. I looked at the 2eme REP, the paratroopers, which I had read about years previously in Murray's book, and decided that was what I would go for. The other regiments in and out of France didn't interest me

A young Belgian lad joined me in a few minutes. We didn't speak but we later became good friends, over the fives years – the minimum contract that you could serve with the Legion. I leafed through some papers on the desk and soon discovered that I could have a pension after 15 years' service with the Legion. But I hadn't planned that far ahead.

I was venturing into the unknown. I was through those gates and I believed I was to be shipped to North Africa for training and subsequent war. But things had changed since the days of Simon Murray. I was going to experience quite a few more small rooms and periods of waiting over the next five years.

We didn't speak as we walked towards the tall locked gates topped with barbed wire. It looked more like a prison wall rather than a passive separation. At the gate I was handed over to a soldier who looked different to the rest. His olive green uniform was tight and neat. I looked at the creases down the back of his legs as I followed. He looked about mid-forty, stocky and he ported a black képi. I later discovered that this was an indication that the wearer was of a certain rank: a chief corporal of at least three years, or the rank of sergeant and above. This one was a chief corporal. I sat in the hallway feeling apprehensive, when a shout that I would soon become familiar with startled me into action.

'Entrez.' The *corporal-chef* (chief corporal) pointed to an open wooden door and I entered. Inside the modern office I was looked up and down. The three gold stripes on the épaulette indicated a captain: he had silver wings and a strip of medals on his chest. Behind me a couple of others stood. I could feel their presence and saw a reflection from the glass cabinet filled with trophies and plaques. The corporal-chef turned and said something to his companion. I was surprised to hear in a broad Geordie accent that seemed somehow strangely foreign a sharp aggressive command.

'Stand straight and face the captain!' I opened my inadequate chest and looked straight at the figure sat in front of me. This seemed to be the correct manner in which to act. I gave my details. There was no requirement to give an address, just my name, nationality, place and date of birth. I was told via the Geordie translator that I was about to sign a contract to serve with the French Foreign Legion for a period of five years after which, if acceptable, this contract could be renewed for further periods of six months to three years. It was slowly beginning to register exactly what I was about to do. I signed the document.

A whistle is blown. The Legion is run on a system of whistles: the first one at 5.30 am for the *réveil* (wake-up call); the second at 6.00 am for *appel* (roll-call); and the third whistle at 6.30 am for *petit déjeuner* (breakfast). It is 12 o'clock – lunch, *déjeuner* or *la soupe*. I've joined behind the others in a queue. Standing outside are another 70 or 80 hopefuls wearing a mixture of uniforms, civilian clothes and green tracksuits. Nerves are beginning to set in. Suddenly, I am surrounded by people but have never felt so alone – they all seem older and different to me. I'm lined up with a crowd of complete strangers of all ages, nationalities and backgrounds.

'A gauche, gauche!'

I turn to the left a while later than the rest and try to keep in step not realizing that everyone else is doing the same, which results in a sea of bobbing heads. The Ordinaire serves a fine selection of inedible delights. I later learn that we are fed anything from sheep brains to chicken stew. I am delighted to find a cockerel's head in my bowl for my first meal. It stays there but the half-decent morsels half-fill my hungry belly, still moaning about the previous night's lack of food!

It may be my pasty white face that reveals my nationality or maybe my lack of dress sense. Regardless, I hear a friendly Welsh voice ask me where I am from. Ray is a 21-year-old ginger-haired hopeful pilot from Wrexham. He almost looks younger than me. That is an achievement in itself! It feels good to hear the voice of someone in the same boat as myself. I soon meet a few more 'Brits'. Ray, Rock and Grant.

A Brit is anyone who speaks English and we soon bond as a mafia, *la mafia Anglaise,* or to the occasional Frenchman *les rosbeef.* The group ensures the protection of the individual. With half a dozen words of French between us, those that have been there longer explain what is happening. There is usually an English-speaking corporal who will also explain, or one of the French speakers. But it doesn't take long to learn the commands that are repeated daily. We soon learn that a whistle means to go outside, that *allez* means go and *en position* means do press-ups.

I was beginning the process of joining. I didn't really know what to expect. We woke at five in the morning to rush outside for *appel.* When we weren't picking up cigarette butts from the floor or washing dishes, we either attended the selection process or trailed around in the rear yard where we would try a few pull-ups. I could only say 'I live at' and count to 20 in French, so I spoke a little with the Spanish speakers instead, my Spanish being a collection of phrases picked up from working with my father in Spain a couple of years previously. Perez chatted to me. He was 28 and a former policeman from Peru with thick bushy black hair and eyebrows to match, but he did not get accepted. Many didn't, as the process was very strict. I wondered if I was the right stuff for this man's army. Everyone seemed so much older and more experienced. Many of them were ex-soldiers from their native countries. And many I think were also lying. Signing the contract I soon discovered didn't mean you were accepted for service. We were required to satisfy a series of prerequisites.

The following morning after *petit dejeuner* we were separated into groups. I was led with a few other men to the medical centre where I spent the whole day in my underpants without being seen. After repeated visits I was given a medical, which included a chest x-ray and an interview with an English-speaking doctor who asked me if I had a *problème sexuele*. Over the next few days I was interviewed and repeatedly asked the same questions in different interviews. I soon discovered that this was to see if the answers corresponded to previous visits. It finally ended with an interview with the *Deuxième Bureau* (French military intelligence), after which I held up a blackboard with my name and number on it while my photograph was taken. I felt like I was in a police line up.

It is generally believed that any crook or maniac can join the Legion and this is not too far from the truth. You have to have a little knowledge and be a good liar if you want to evade the red tape. If you are wanted for a crime, either in your own country or by Interpol, you have two choices. Lie and get found out at a later date and all your hard work in the Legion will end in a good beating, a bit of time *en taule* (an unpleasant experience in a Legion prison) and a rapid exit without a handshake back to the street. Tell the truth and depending on your crime the Legion may decide to keep you, change your identity with a false name and deny your presence to all who enquire about you, including your family.

It soon became apparent that there was a system to joining the Legion. We started dressed in our civilian clothes in which we passed though the gates. As we progressed through the joining process we went from civilian clothes to green tracksuits. Down in the cellar we handed in all our possessions – so long as you succeeded in being accepted to the Legion you were sure never to see your possessions again. This was in fact a good system: no matter how rich or poor you were, or what title or profession you held on the outside, once inside those gates we were all equal. From that moment forward only who you were and how you acted determined what your life would be like – slacken off, steal or worse and you were sure to regret it! Fortunately, I didn't have any possessions. So in exchange for my clothes I was given a green tracksuit, five disposable Bic razors, some shaving cream and a bar of *savon de Marseille* (pure soap).

I would use the savon to shower and wash my clothes. I didn't need to use the shaving things yet. The luxury of washing machines and tumble driers was something I would not have from that day on – everything would be washed by hand.

To keep us occupied during the process and to take full advantage of our presence we were routinely sent to different jobs in the camp. After breakfast, some stayed behind to wash the dishes and clean the floors. Others at times were sent to work with the Képi Blanc and some were sent out of camp to Poloubier (the foreign Legion retirement home). Schmitt, a pale plump German came back one evening full of smiles and stories:

'I have met my countrymen today.'

The silence among the listeners was complimentary. 'I met soldiers from the Second World War – veterans of the Waffen-SS. Forty-five years on and they are still here! They are finished with the Legion and are, how you say? – "long holidays". They are fighting in Vietnam, Indo China and Algeria. Now all they do is make wine and souvenirs for the Legion. They are always drunk and they never leave. But good news! At Christmas the Legion buys hookers from Marseille for the *Anciens* [retired legionnaires]. I can't wait to get old!'

As I went though the process I was promoted from tracksuit to uniform, and in the tradition of all armies I went to have my hair shaved off. I wasn't too worried about this but one of the other men in the queue, a Sikh, seemed agitated, to the point that he was held down by the corporals to cut his hair. It seems that the often-aggressive sense of humour found among most soldiers was not lost in the Legion. A couple of hours after his haircut the man was told that he was not accepted and sent on his way.

John, a Dutchman, was called to the 'BALE' – the former legionnaire's office where the corporal-chef pulled out a dusty folder and showed it to him. He was amazed to see a very much younger looking father and five-year contract.

'Well, I do remember my dad speaking some foreign language years ago as a small child, but I had no idea he was in the Legion,' he commented in a heavy accent.

I attended an intelligence test in a large classroom. The corporal played a cassette with the instructions and for the next hour I looked at puzzles, did maths problems and answered questions about word associations and meanings, the results of which would determine my career in the Legion. I was also given an aptitude test for Morse code, which I did very well at: unfortunate, as I had to spend the next two years trying to avoid becoming a signaller.

Red Tab Day! I was given a red tab. When we had been given a uniform we wore a green tab, which meant you were on you way to being accepted. Promotion from green to red meant that you were going on to training. I would shortly be leaving for Castelnaudary. I was in. I was soon to learn that evening what it meant to be 'in'. That lunchtime a Polish man was tasked to work in the Ordinaire. During the slack period between lunch and supper he spent most of his time crawling on all fours to the wine machine (forbidden to us lowlifes!). Within a couple of hours the old bloke (he was about 35) was well and truly singing to the fishes and not surprisingly found himself in front of the captain. The captain had his say before quite unceremoniously slapping the 'Polack' around the face who happily returned the favour. All was not well.

That evening news of the incident with the Pole, who was still surprisingly unmarked, was whispered in small groups. The next day he was to be dismissed so that night he was punished. We, the chosen red tabs, were to impose that punishment. The corporals briefed us and later that evening when he went for his evening toilet we followed the unfortunate man. We were given the nod from the corporal and silently moved behind him: 12 chosen tough men to sort out a minor discipline problem. I was the youngest of the 12 and a little unsure of myself. A large Frenchman grabbed him by the neck and smashed his head against the toilet door. Another punched him and someone else kicked him to the floor. I did put the boot in even though I quite liked the guy while the other men who were more experienced went to town and painted it red.

My selection had been quick at about four weeks. We attended a visit to the museum that exhibited many artefacts, uniforms and weapons from the Legion's 150-year history. The Legion was created on 10 March 1831 by King Louis Philippe, after thousand of troops of mixed nationalities from the Napoleonic campaigns were brawling on the streets of Paris. It was formed to give them something to fight for – the occupation of Algeria. In 1835 the Legion was given to the Spanish monarch to help fight the insurrection in Spain. In the same year a second Legion was created, which continued the Algerian campaign through to the 20th century. This is the Legion that exists today.

I looked through the glass at the wooden hand of Captaine Danjou, a legendary legionnaire who along with 63 men fought a losing battle against the 2,000 Mexican soldiers surrounding the village where they had taken shelter in 1863. Danjou was killed; the only part later recovered of his body was his wooden hand, a souvenir from a previous battle. The five remaining legionnaires, out of water, food and ammo, bayonet charged the Mexicans. Two were killed and the others spared for their bravery. Each year the battle is commemorated with a parade and a party. In front of this hand I listened to a recording in the languages of everyone present explaining our contract.

Within days I found myself in Castelnaudary, a small town near the Pyrenees, which is where the 4th Foreign Regiment is based. When I arrived the camp was modern and immaculate. Four new barrack blocks framed a well-swept tarmac parade square. It was hardly what I expected, and seemed a far call from the muddy tents in the Debel Mountains of Africa that I had read about. Rock, Ray and Grant were still with me, and it felt good to have some people from a common background to talk to.

This was where our training and indoctrination began. Forget all those nights on the town, forget your car, civilian clothes and designer labels, your bank accounts and credit cards, forget your brothers, fathers, mothers and sisters, forget that broken-hearted girl you left a thousand miles away, forget your kids, forget your videos and remote controlled televisions, forget you ever existed. From now on your body and mind belong to the Legion so you had better get used to it! Freedom of choice didn't exist here: if you wanted a piss you needed to ask, if you leant upon a wall you did press-ups, seniors where always right and never to be questioned. Within a few weeks I wouldn't want to make a decision without asking permission since initiative wasn't encouraged. Well, not for the moment. We didn't go anywhere without being accompanied by a grown-up.

Over the next week we started learning; from five o'clock each morning and ending around 11 each night. We learnt songs and the slow eight-eight paces to the minute drill march – around forty paces a minute slower than most armies' marches. It was extremely difficult to walk this slowly. If we got it wrong we ran as a squad around the camp and did press-ups. We always got it wrong. It would take months to get it right, and half of us didn't speak a word of French. We were taught from a basic level: how to fold clothes, how our lockers had to look. Everything had to be immaculate. Each morning before six we would be washed shaved, beds undone with blankets folded, rooms and washrooms cleaned. At six there was the roll-call. Downstairs dressed in running kit, then straight to activities. Sometimes it would be marching, sometimes vaccinations; there was always something to do until breakfast at seven. Breakfast was dry bread with jam and coffee – the corner stone of any hard day's activities.

It was half-past seven and once again I was on parade for the morning run. The run was about eight miles and it was just a case of trying to keep up. Fortunately, I was a good runner (most probably due to my measly ten-and-a-half stone) and I generally kept at the front until the end. All the runs were followed by the usual sits-ups, pull-ups and six-metre rope. The rope had to be climbed without use of the legs. We were shown a technique in which the opposing leg to the arm that pulled was raised which helped some a great deal. But it didn't help me. I could only make it halfway up.

We worked every day. For the next four months there would be no days off. Sunday evening we packed our *sac à dos* (backpack) for the following day's march to the 'farm'. The farm was where the corporals and sergeants had their own way. We would stay at the farm for a month, but first we had to walk there. We had been divided into *groupes de combat*. These were eight- to ten-man patrols that included two corporals and a sergeant to lead. I was with the group of Sgt Pellier. He was a heavily built Frenchman who seemed to hate everything and everyone. He never spoke to us. The only reaction he would give to acknowledge our existence was a deep grunt and a sharp punch in the shoulder or at times around the head. One of the corporals was a tall, proud ginger Scottish fellow. Cpl Bruce was formerly in the Scottish Guards and would ensure I understood what was going on.

It is difficult to imagine how so many people without a common language can be trained. There is usually a wide variety of languages in a Legion *section* (platoon). In the case of basic training there is usually someone who can translate. Of course those who spoke with more obscure tongues would have to be shown by actions, mimics, diagrams, pictures drawn in the dirt with sticks or in the good old-fashioned Legion manner: beaten until he just nods his head! We were given French lessons, which were usually done by the platoon commander. To help us learn our French we were partnered off with a *bonhomme* (buddy). This was usually a French speaker. I was partnered up with a 25-year-old, well-built Italian goat herder who seemed to have it all downstairs and not much up top. Over the next four months I would grow to detest Stabia. But for the time being I had to learn French and stick with him night and day – we would be forced to be inseparable. Wherever he went I would have to go and vice versa. Like two convicts chained together this would go on – to the toilet, to the shower, to meals and so on.

So Monday morning we stood outside the cookhouse dressed in our olive green uniforms ready to go. I looked around at the others. Ray grinned. He was excited to get out of the camp and start the 'real' stuff. In the background I could hear a platoon singing a slow song:

Contre les Viets, contre l'ennemi
Partout où le devoir fait signe
Soldats de France, soldats de pays,
Nous remonterons vers les lignes.

Against the Vietnamese, against the enemy
Wherever we have to go
Soldiers of France, soldiers of our country,
We all line up for battle.

The crystal-blue sky promised a fine day and the air was already warming up. I was looking forward to getting stuck into a few hills. I enjoyed walking and running. It dispelled my anger and calmed me down. We each carried a Famas (the French 5.56-calibre assault rifle), a heavy sac à dos and *l'équipement* – a webbing consisting of six magazines, a water bottle and mug and a rifle-cleaning kit. Some of us were given extra equipment to carry: the vhf radios that weighed 10 kilos, the 7.5-calbre AA50 machine-gun or the personal radios that were like a couple of bricks stuck together but only a little heavier. These personal radios had to be worn by a thin strap around the neck. After a long day with this hanging off you, your bottom lip truly did reach the floor! In a long column we set off, each man with his rifle slung over his right shoulder. We did not patrol. We didn't know any tactics. We just marched, and when the Legion marches it lives up to its motto 'march or die'. We left the security of the camp and headed for the hills.

By nine o'clock the sun was warm on my face and sweat seeped into my shirt. I could begin to feel the webbing rub, and my mouth began to dry. The single water bottle we carried would have to last us until the first water point. Water conservation was something that soon became second nature. Physiologically, the body needs to replace the water it sweats. Without this replacement the body deteriorates, it becomes weak; you get headaches, light-headedness, vomiting which leads to further dehydration, which leads eventually to unconsciousness and death. During the marches we would only be allowed to drink when we were told and we were always told not to drink too much. I was taught 'the more you drink the more you sweat' and so I never became a great guzzler of water. I must have spent every march in a constant state of headaches and giddiness and yet my body still kept going.

In the mid-afternoon we stopped outside a derelict farmhouse and cooked some rations. I picked up a couple of pebbles, placed them around a small white firelighter and heated a tin of pork and lentils while I ate the two dry crackers with jam for starters. Twenty-four hours' rations at that time in France consisted of one tin as a main meal, crackers and either tuna or sardines, four boiled sweets, one coffee, a hot chocolate, a packet of soup, jam and a bar of chocolate. Gradually, through the months we all, unsurprisingly, lost weight. Some of the men complained of sore feet, but they were ignored. You don't complain. You just get on with it. You won't find a sympathetic ear in the Legion. You are most likely to get a punch around the ear and a string of obscenities spat in your face.

We stopped in a small village and moved into the shade. One by one we filled our bottles from the tap next to an old well. The red brick from the buildings had fallen on the path. An old lady wearing a dark shawl cradled a basket of vegetables and asked us if we wanted to buy any. The sergeant dismissed her with a shooing motion of his hand. She shrugged and slowly walked back to her house.

We didn't see anyone else in the village. The calm silence between the buildings soothed my mind. I could feel the weight leave my feet as I rested. The little moments of calm in these rural places made me smile and appreciate the throbbing pains in my feet. It made it more real and worthwhile. A flickering light caught my eye through the shutters that had lost their paint. Inside the old lady had lit a fire. I wondered why as the day was warm. She looked lonely.

We arrived at the farm towards the late afternoon. I'd had a long day, walking 28 kilometres. Yet this was most certainly the shortest and easiest march that I would do in the Legion.

The farm nestled in rolling hills and beech woods. We stayed in the barn and slept on camp beds while the corporals, sergeants and the lieutenant stayed in the farmhouse building. We settled down for the night but not before a couple of lessons and a long singing session. I didn't really see the point in learning all these songs. I didn't understand its relevance to being a soldier. I knew it was a tradition, but why adopt a style of life from our predecessors simply because that was the way they lived? I questioned the old stuff until it proved itself to me: I didn't think singing the songs brought us together. It didn't create camaraderie. Hardship, shared lifestyles and equality made us bond. Songs made us hoarse. It began to annoy me.

The following morning we paraded at half-past five. The sun was just beginning to creep over the hills and the air was damp but fresh. After roll-call we went behind the barn to shave in the long steel troughs with taps that were fed from a single pipe. They looked like raised cattle feed trays. It was in these that we would wash and do our laundry. We shaved every morning. There weren't any mirrors, which at first took a little getting used to. A year or two later I got into the habit of feeling for stubble and aiming for it by following my fingers with my razor. But for the moment I went through the motions not really cutting anything away! The water was cold. When I splashed it on my face it slapped me into consciousness and shooed away my sleep. I approached the sergeant and asked permission to go to the toilet. *Permission de pisser* was granted and with my bonhomme metaphorically chained to my ankle we went to the toilet. This was a wooden shed in which a large pit was dug under the floor. The centre of the floor boasted a square hole over which you had to squat and hope for the best. At first my aim wasn't really that good to begin with but as time went on I did manage to avoid soiling around the hole.

Before breakfast we had the *apéritif*; a few press-ups followed by climbing up the rope and sit-ups. This was the same for every meal and the given system for many daily routines in the Legion. It was generally during courses, although I did find myself doing this in everyday life according to the regiment and the company. It's surprising how a little done often, can make a great deal of difference most of the time.

After the morning run we started the day's lessons. We were taught how to patrol the surrounding countryside: how to change the formation of the patrol from two columns to arrowhead or single file. This was done in silence with the use of hand signals. We learnt how to read maps, take bearings and pace 100 metres, which would help us judge how far we had travelled. My 55 paces for 100 metres never changed throughout my military career. We learned how to camouflage our features to break up the obvious shape of the head and shoulders. With a drop of water from our *bidon* (water bottle) we would mix up a muddy paste and smear it over our faces, necks and hands. Cosmetic camouflage sticks would have to wait until we got to our regiments. We patrolled and came under fire, dashing into cover before returning fire to the enemy. The enemy was always *les Russes* (the Russians). The corporals and sergeants acted out examples of how to act and how to react. A corporal patrolled with his helmet off and his weapon flailing around. This was an example of how not to do things.

We had a large, overweight American in our section. He was always the last one to come in from the morning run and he continuously complained. One evening he showed me a blank round that he had found.

'I'm keeping this just in case. I'm going to shoot that fucking sergeant.' He never did get to frighten the sergeant with a loud bang. However, later that night when he was on sentry he made the grave mistake of deserting. Packed with a water bottle and his French assault rifle he wandered into the night. The following morning a commotion started with the instructors. Hands were waved and questions asked to the French lads, particularly the American's French bonhomme, who was on sentry with him the night he left.

We carried on training as usual. In the mid-afternoon we paraded back at the farm. Something was said that I couldn't understand but it was obvious from the actions of the *sergent-chef* (staff sergeant) that it was a warning. A grey Renault 5 pulled into the farm and two heavily built Tahitians stepped into view. They were part of the Legion military police.

They were a law to themselves. You did not want to be put in a Legion prison, particularly in Castelnaudary. As the speech went on the police opened up the boot of the car. A well-beaten head slowly edged into view. I could hardly recognize the features of the fat American trussed up like a Christmas turkey in the boot. Nobody else tried to desert from that day on. Those who wished to leave would just have to wait until training was over.

Three weeks later we once again saw the American back in the camp. He was no longer overweight but drawn and haggard. He reminded me of a photograph I had seen of the POW camps in Germany during the Second World War. The *taule* (military prison) in the training regiment was not a pleasant experience. The American was beaten most days and he was fed very little. The usual mealtime experience for him was to be told he was a *gros porc* or big pig, and have his food thrown on the floor. Like an animal he would scoop it up in his hands to eat. During the day the prisoners swept the floors and did chores around the camp. They also had to run everywhere. We would often see them being punished around the camps, pushing out the press-ups and doing forward rolls on the tarmac roads.

During the time on the farm I began to get to know some of the other recruits. We had very little spare time. If we weren't training we were singing. The songs were slow like the slow march of the Legion. I didn't understand the words so I just mimicked the sounds. The songs reminded me of ancient monks singing deep laborious hymns. But still every now and then we would stop and I would chat to the others. Syan was a skinny Syrian formerly in his native army. He had fine smooth Arabic features without stubble. He was a few years older than me and we seemed to get on fine. As we stopped to make coffee or sip water he would tell me about the Syrian army and his family back home. He had a wife and a daughter. I wondered why he was here but I didn't like to ask. A legionnaire's past is rarely a subject of conversation.

Belge, who had been with me from the day I joined, spoke a little English. He was always smiling. He would call me by my first name, which was generally not accepted in the Legion. We were always known by our surnames. We would address each other with brash, sharp French. But for the moment we were really still civilians and we still had our civilian traits, and I was Tony and he was Belge. Belge had been in the Belgian commandos but had to be released early for some reason. He was a good friend. He wanted to be a paratrooper, as did I.

There were three other English-speaking lads in the section. Ray was still with me having made it through the joining process. I have yet to meet another man who was so relaxed about everything. His round ginger face was always smiling as he nonchalantly went about his business as if he didn't have a care in the world. Here we were starting a journey into the unknown away from everything we had previously known and there he was with a cheesy grin continuously mimicking the instructor and making fun of the whole thing.

Rock was 24 years old and from London. He was the only person in the section to actually put on weight during basic training. Rock would not take any abuse from anyone and he had a rather interesting philosophy of justice. He told us about a little justice he did of his own. Outside his house in east London a few boys were playing football. The ball landed in the garden next door and the kids were trying to get it back from the owner. The owner blatantly refused to return the ball. Rock thought this to be a miscarriage of justice so in his own words:

'So, I grabbed this geezer by the fucking neck and there was this gate post so I just smashed his head on it, but the fucking cunt just fucking laughed so I smashed it again and again until he stopped laughing and gave the fucking ball back – what a fucking wanker!'

Rock really didn't like his French bonhomme – a wiry slimy man covered in acne. So one morning in the tradition of his name he took him to the side and beat him on the head with a large stone, which we all thought to be highly amusing – I hardly think the Frenchman deserved this treatment but the Legion can be a tough place. Nobody really messed with Rock. He was always jovial and ready to amuse. He couldn't speak French so to keep people amused he would mimic animals with his hands and create strange animals noises – ants would squeak and buffalos would growl. This kept the sergeants highly amused and for brief moments we could forget the training and the regime and relax into what everyday life in the Legion could be like. Then someone would jump up, bark an order and we would be back to patrolling and sweating. Rock's father was a member of the IRA but he really didn't care; he was a Londoner. He spoke like a Londoner and was ashamed that his old man had helped to bomb an English hotel.

Grant was from Southern Ireland. He had dark southern European features and had spent some time in the Irish army. He was the only one among the four of us that had any previous military experience so he would continuously compare what we did to what he had previously learnt.

The time at the farm passed quickly. We were far too busy to allow it to drag. Once a week we would march the 28 kilometres back to the camp where we could have a meagre fresh meal and get to run around the assault course. Food was something we didn't get much of so we were continuously hungry. I would try to fill up on bread, and when a shout for *rabe* (extra) was called by the chefs we would go up for more.

These marches back and forth strengthened us for the *Képi Blanc* march. This was to be at the end of the month at the farm. It was a three-day march during which we would go 120 kilometres around the surrounding hills. Once this march was completed we would be given our famous Képi Blanc. During the first week in the camp we had been preparing for this. We had ironed our parade uniforms to the immaculate state required by the corporals. The insignia badges had to be stitched on and creases put in the front and rear of the shirt. Each crease had to be sharp and in a straight line. No *double plis* (double creases), and no overlapping of creases. Above each front pocket of the shirt three creases would run vertically from the épaulette. The creases had to be exactly 35 millimetres apart. The back of the shirt boasted two horizontal creases with three vertical creases joining them. These had to be 53 millimetres apart. We spent hours getting it right. Each time the corporals would measure the creases and inspect each surface of the shirt for unwanted folds or blemishes.

We learnt how to present ourselves to the senior ranks: first a knock on the door and request to enter. Then a slow march into the room, halting to attention, a salute, always looking the senior in the eyes, and the well-rehearsed lines:

'Engage Volontaire Sloane, un mois de service, Troisieme Compagnie, Section de Lieutenant Herve a vos ordres caporal.' 'Engaged Volunteer [I was not yet a legionnaire] Sloane, one month of service, Third Company, Lieutenant Herve's platoon at your orders corporal.' A stony uncomfortable silence would follow before being told to stand at ease. Once again a rehearsed line:

'I put myself at ease at your orders, sir'. Of course we were never really at ease.

Blanc Marche was about to start. We were assembled outside the farm in a field. Our rucksacks were packed with three days' rations, our tents, radios, sleeping bags and weapons. We distributed out our weight equally with our bonhommes. Stabia was to carry the 10 kilogram radio so I took his tent parts, rations and sleeping bag. A couple of minutes before we were due to depart we found the radio to be broken. It was too late to hand back his belongings so we just carried on. This big muscular Italian had the build but he did not have the heart.

Within the first few miles as the sun was beginning to blind our eyes and the sweat began to soak through our shirts to our rucksacks he began to moan. And the moaning would not stop for three days! If our buddies could not carry their equipment then it was up to their bonhomme to get them through the march. This was hardly fair but I suppose it was to build solidarity between us, but I just ended up detesting the man. I already had most of his kit but there I was pushing him with one hand up the hill. We began to fall behind. Belge dropped back to help. Belge always helped. The corporal told me to take Stabia's webbing and then his rifle. My head down, sweat stinging my eyes I listened to my heavy, rasped breath and persevered.

The pace was slow but continuous. We finished marching in the early evening each night. There was always enough light to go and collect wood for a bonfire. But before that we had to construct the camp. We each carried two *toiles de tente* – two canvas triangular tent cloths which were attached by metal buttons on the edges. On one side it was desert brown and on the other camouflage. We also each carried eight iron tent pegs. To hold the tent erect we each had two wooden tent poles. The canvases once attached made a pyramid shape, which was held in the centre by the four pole attachments. The whole edifice was pinned down with the pegs. We placed our ponchos on the floor as ground sheets. These were a course green plastic, which in wet weather we used in the traditional sense – slipping our heads through the centre and having the canopy drape around out bodies. In the rain we would look like green ghosts slowly marching, singing morbid songs about death and being lost souls.

The platoon consisted of three *groupes de combat*. The three groups made up three sides of a square and the fourth was the command element – in this case all the sergeants and instructors. The tents all had to form a precise square. Like primitive architects we aligned the sides of the tents with lengths of string. If it wasn't straight we would have to take them all down and start again. It would take a frustrating couple of hours to set up camp. But it would eventually be a perfect square of canvas pyramids.

Then we built the fire and sang before mounting a guard for the night. It all seemed very old-fashioned for 1989. I was travelling back in time. For the evening meal the sergent-chef collected items from our rations – sweets, biscuits, coffee, main meals and chocolate – which he then mixed in a large pot with boiling water. We ate this sloppy gruel every night and had the runs every day! The following morning we shaved and washed in our mess tins before a breakfast of two dry biscuits with a sachet of jam washed down with black coffee. The French don't have milk in their coffee; neither did they drink tea, so neither could be found in the ration boxes.

We didn't know where we were going on the marches; we just followed the man in front which was demoralizing, never knowing when we were going to stop and never being told how much further to go. The lieutenant would lead the way. One evening I saw the officer empty his sac à dos: inside he had a polystyrene sleeping mat padded out with a sleeping bag to give the illusion of a full and heavy rucksack. He collected his tent and rations from the four-tonne wagon that always seemed to be wherever we stopped. I lost respect for all officers in the Legion from that moment.

There are two ways to become an officer in the Legion: either you are French and you spend five years at the Fountainebleau Officer Academy and you finish near the top, or if you are a legionnaire, you can work your way through the ranks until you are eventually commissioned. These were the officers that we respected: the ones who were legionnaires heart and soul. I always found it ironic that the strict discipline in the Legion that enabled the French officers to easily command and be treated apart was not in fact genuine respect, just discipline. I never met a single legionnaire who truly respected a career officer who was not a legionnaire; they didn't leave their entire previous life behind them to become something unique. They were French army dressed up as Legion soldiers. And they didn't carry their weight but they could always run like whippets.

I shouldn't be too harsh. They had their job to do as discipliners and they were good at it – that was not in question. Although I didn't respect them, others may have done. Respect and discipline are two different issues: you can do as you are told without having to respect the person you are obeying. The officers in the Legion only spend two years in a posting and are never permanently attached to a Legion unit. They may serve and return, but never stay unless they have been promoted through the ranks from legionnaire.

The Legion has strict discipline. There is no doubt that the reasons why legionnaires do what they do are not their own. They obey orders without question. They are indoctrinated to do as the Legion pleases without question. We were not thinking soldiers – we just obeyed. I once read the memoirs of a legionnaire who made a final attack on an enemy position. Once the position was clear he was asked how many bullets he had remaining. He had none. When questioned about how many he had before the attack, he said, 'I didn't have any!' He went to battle because he was told to.

The Legion is isolated. Once inside those gates you can forget the rest of the world. I used to think and look at the stars and wonder about my own existence, wonder about God and evolution, about 'it' and what 'it' is all about. I wrote poetry about this and sat and wondered. After a few months in the Legion the only thoughts in my head were when was I going to get my next sexual encounter, my next drink, and would I ever get to kill somebody, as this was getting frustrating? Reflecting upon this now, the Legion has the ideal cannon fodder soldiers. A legionnaire has no family only the Legion, he has no bank, no car, no house, no civilian clothing, he can't get married in the first five years and then he has to ask permission, he can't go anywhere – he has the Legion. The Legion is his pride, his mates and his family. He will do whatever the Legion commands. He will fight. He will die; because that is all he has.

We marched behind the officer. The Italian moaned and the tall Polish guy swore.

'Fucking hell, shit!'

I remember on the final hill of the second day looking back towards the rest. One of the Frenchmen was struggling. He had been struggling for hours. And the corporals were irate. My head turned to the sound of English voices.

'Get up you lazy twat, you fucking fat fuck, get your fucking arse up!' Corporal Johnston began to punch the man in the face. I found it ironic that the corporal doing the beating was a British police officer before he joined. It's amazing how a few years within a particular environment can change you from one person to another. It's crazy how the mind is a sponge and we all soak up the suds and the dirt (unless of course you are aware that this is happening, then you may be able to absorb only the suds).

He put his hands up to protect himself but this just made his aggressor angrier. More shouts. More screams. I felt nothing for the Frenchman. No sympathy. No guilt at not helping him. I just felt disgust – if you can't take the pace then you should not have joined. This was the Foreign Legion – you know its reputation, especially being French. What did you expect – massages and French maids throwing themselves at you because you were in the Legion? You have to work for that! And you wouldn't get much time for that if you stayed either!

I can't remember the end of the Képi Blanc Marche. It was hard but it would prove to be a walk in the park compared to the other stuff I would have to do. It was still quite an achievement considering most of us were straight from the streets and we were only four weeks into our training.

.... CHAPTER 3

We were back in the camp and our pale desert coloured uniforms were ready. We had rehearsed the lines we were required to recite, and we could sing a couple of songs. We were ready to receive the coveted képi blanc. We marched to the rear of the officer's mess, which was the most architecturally appropriate place for the ceremony. We wore our crisp uniforms with pride. I looked across to Ray, who had lost a little weight, and winked. The red tassels hanging from his green épaulettes fluttered in the light breeze. The wide-blue cloth belt, the cummerbund, wrapped tightly around me felt like a tourniquet, but it was the traditional uniform. Over this wrap I wore a green staple belt from which my bayonet frog dangled. We stood in three ranks in front of an old stone arch with elegant pillars that reminded me of Roman architecture. Four rifles were placed in front of us, creating a wigwam of metal and plastic. From the barrel of the supporting centre rifle the *compagnie* flag, a bright yellow touched on the edges by red braid, gently flapped in the light breeze. In front of this we stood proud.

We recited the *Code d'Honneur* (the Legion Code of Honour). We didn't swear allegiance to a monarchy as in England – we swore to serve France, and to be impartial to all legionnaires regardless of race, creed or religion. We swore to always be clean, smart and to hold ourselves proud as legionnaires. We swore to respect our enemy, never to leave our injured or dead, and never to surrender. We donned our white képis and marched away back to the classroom where we were allowed to drink a couple of beers. Belge drank as much as he could in as short as time as possible but the corporals turned a blind eye. Forty-five minutes of beers and songs was swiftly followed by a quick exit to our room to prepare for the next phase of training. We were legionnaires.

For the next three or four weeks we trained in camp. I was beginning to wish we were back on the farm. Before breakfast we had the apéritif. Each spare minute of the day we marched around the camp and sang songs. If we got it wrong we would run and then do press-ups. We always got it wrong. We always had to wear the Famas (a 5.56-calibre assault rifle) around our necks, which was held by a thin strap that weighed against the neck and got in the way. I really hated this part of training. Continuously, we were punished. Continuously, we ran and did press-ups.

If we had a little time free we would sit on the balcony and chat while always giving the impression we were actively doing something useful like hanging out washing or polishing boots. This was another chance to talk to the other legionnaires. Swartz was in his early twenties.

'Polish border is guarded by armed men ... I had to be quick. I waited until nightfall before I went for it.' He had escaped the Iron Curtain as did all the Eastern Bloc lads in the Legion at the time.

'Rat tat-tat-tat-tat-tat.' He shook his left hand while demonstrating with the other how he steered the jeep that he had stolen from the Polish Army.

'Moi … comme ça.' Ducking low, his arms flailed over his head to show where the rounds the guard fired at him went. I looked at his tanned tight inset cheeks. His jaw was clenched as he relived the experience. He spoke seven languages and had scored 100 percent in his Niveau Général test, the intelligence test we had taken in Aubagne when joining. When he arrived at the Legion gates he still had the Uzi (Israeli submachine gun) and stolen jeep. There were many characters in the Legion and just as many men of character.

We did the assault course a few times a week. Each time we were taught a new technique to conquer an obstacle. I rolled on my belly over the top rung of the rope ladder. A couple of rungs further down I swung out and landed like a cat on the next obstacle. The two logs were soon left behind as I dove under the wire fence. It hung 12 inches above a 12-metre slab of concrete. Each technique was taught to conserve energy. I pushed with both legs and slid rather than crawled to the end. We didn't put one hand in front of the other to pull ourselves forward, rather we slid our palms along the smooth concrete as if polishing it. This conserved our strength. We jumped down holes and swung over planks. Once we knew each obstacle we would be tested on our times. The assault course was fast and tiring; three and a half minutes of anaerobic pain! After the first two obstacles I could not breathe. It reminded me of being in the gas chamber and trying to breathe CS gas during our nuclear, biological and chemical warfare lessons. Suddenly, my lungs could not work although they tried desperately. It was this uncomfortable feeling of suffocation for three minutes. At the end I slumped forward to catch my breath but it was too quick and soon evaded me. I wiped the sweat from my eyes and started to jog. The sergeant was calling me to the grenade throwing practice.

We marched back to camp. We entered through the gates singing a German song, although at the time I did not understand the lyrics:

Im Hafen kehren die Legionäre
bei der Schwarzen Rose ein.
Sie pfeiffen auf Geld und Ruhm und Ehre
Denn schon bald kann alles anders sein.

I later discovered that the song is in outmoded German, and translates something as follows:

At the harbour the legionnaires
go to the Black Rose.
They don't care about money, fame or honour
Because soon everything can change.

The sentinel snapped to attention as the officers passed and saluted. The 'taulers' were brought to attention by the corporal-chef in charge. I saw the, once fat, American among them with a paintbrush in his hand. A general was visiting and the grass wasn't green enough so they were painting it greener! The job reminded me of a few months previously when I was renting a caravan on the outskirts of Cambridge for a few months. I answered an advert in a shop window and received bizarre instructions to wait outside a pub at six o'clock on Monday morning. Monday morning came and I sat waiting with a rough looking bunch of lads wearing heavy scruffy coats and boots. I was dropped off in a field with a hoe and spent the next 12 hours weeding a field of onions. It was one of the most tedious things I have ever done. The next day I went again but this time I was in the back of a trailer being pulled by a tractor up and down a potato field. Four of us stood facing each other for the next 12 hours separating mud from potatoes on a conveyor belt. It was the very tedious things in life that made me restless. Friday came and I decided to ask the boss about my wages, which were cash in hand. He leant over to me, with a roll-up hanging from his bearded mouth, close to my ear – where I could smell the beer on his breath – and gave me instructions in a deep hoarse voice:

'Meet me in the Dobblers at seven aclack fu ya munnay.' I bustled through the crowded smoky back room of the pub and found him sitting in the corner. We met at the bar and he discreetly handed me 100 quid and told me to get the beers in.

The little pointless things in the Legion made me question if this was really what I wanted to do. Once during my five years I had thought of deserting, of returning back to England because of the seemingly meaningless jobs. However, it was my personal pride that kept me for the duration. I thought, how could I return and hold my head high or even mention the Legion if I deserted? I would not be able to without having the feeling that people would think that it was too difficult for me: that I was not tough enough. I have since often seen articles in magazines in which a 'deserter' has written about the Legion and put it down. When people fail at something they tend to put that very thing down to compensate for their own failure. Make excuses. Men who have the courage and determination to finish their contract, to keep to their word and signature, rarely dirty the Legion name. At least if they did they would have earned the right to. They would have done their time and earned the right to state an opinion.

We marched to the armoury to collect our rifles and then to the 200-metre indoor *champ de tire* (shooting range). When we were not shooting we were lying outside practising. The corporals put a cleaning rod in the barrel upon which a one franc piece was balanced. If we pulled the trigger and the coin fell we would do press-ups. I wasn't a great shot but I was good at press-ups.

This was a busy time. We attended lessons about nuclear, biological and chemical weapons:

'Gaz, gaz, gaz!' I dropped to one knee, squeezed my eyes shut and held my breath. I frantically struggled to open the pouch to my *appareil normal de protection* (gas mask) and placed it over my head. I shouted out 'Gaz, gaz, gaz' to dispel any gas still within the mask. This was an annoying thing to do in the summer heat. The NBC, (nuclear, biological and chemical protection) uniforms were hot and sticky and if we were not quick enough we had to run around the block.

We learnt about the rifle and its parts, its weight loaded and unloaded, and its length. I wondered about the rationale behind all of these details. Did I need to know how long the rifle was in order to shoot straight? Did it matter that I knew I was carrying a 76-centimetre length of metal and plastic weighing 3.61 kilos? I could understand why I needed to know the radios and their frequencies. But the trivia was frustrating, as was learning dozens of marching songs. I didn't see the point. But that is Legion life to begin with. I would soon discover that there was far more to it that running around doing pointless little tasks. One day I would even enjoy singing the odd song.

The 4th Foreign Legion Regiment (4eme RE) was responsible for training. It was here where legionnaires would return to do promotion courses. The first promotion course was the CME (Certificat Militaire Elementaire – Advanced Military Certificate), which was needed to become a corporal. This was about two months long and was run in the old camp, which was formerly a prison in the town of Castelnaudary and not a great deal had changed since then. To get promoted to sergeant another course was needed – CM1 (Certificat Militaire Niveau 1 – Military Certificate Level 1) – six months of pure torment! The 4eme RE also trained the signallers and medics who practised on us. We needed to have the necessary inoculations so frequently we were marched to the medical centre to act as guinea pigs. The vaccinations were injected into the sub-cutaneous tissue under the shoulder blade. Sometimes they would take blood, using syringes, which was often a messy business. The medical centre had its own fair share of casualties to deal with. One of these was Schmitt:

Schmitt looked like a pig. He had a round full face and small demon eyes. He was a little overweight for his 20 years. I didn't really like the man, there just seemed to be something not right. He was with us for a few weeks. After réveil at around five-thirty in the morning we shaved. Ray arrived first one morning to find the toilet floor covered in a huge pool of blood. The cubicle door was locked so he climbed over the top to find Schmitt slumped on the floor. He had sliced his wrists. Of course, the medics were called and he was taken away. I mopped up the blood that had been trodden around the room: nice red boot prints circled around the sinks before disappearing up the corridor. It reminded me of when I was a small child. We used to make stamps with potatoes and make our own patterns with them. Fortunately, or unfortunately for Schmitt, he didn't die and so once he was patched up he was sentenced to the usual month in prison before being released back to the streets.

The company was paraded by the sergeant major, who was not happy. Stern words were said but the interesting part was the explanation of how to kill oneself correctly. He didn't care if you wanted to finish 'it' (whatever 'it' was) off but just make sure you do it properly so as to not waste people's time.

'Don't cut the wrist; cut down the inside of the elbows deep – there are bigger veins and you will have more success.'

He demonstrated with elaborate hand gestures so that we were all sure.

*

We travelled in the back of four-tonne wagons with our rifles between our legs for seven hours to Camerac, a small hamlet near the Pyrenees. It was ideal for a little extra marching! We arrived and were accommodated in another farmhouse. The Legion must own half the farms in France as we seemed to spend a great deal of time in them. We slept up in the attic on camp beds.

Early the next morning the whistle blew. We jumped out of bed and quickly dressed before diving through the small window onto the fireman's pole and sliding down to the parade square. No matter where the Legion was you would always find a parade square usually made from rocks painted white. We spent the day preparing for a few days' marching in the mountains. We set off in the usual manner – one long line with our bonhommes. I had Stabia yet again. Back in the camp he used to masturbate in the dead of night in the bunk above me, so the farm was a chance to catch up on some sleep! For some reason I was given an extra rifle to carry – one of the spares. I also had a personal radio. This was an old-fashioned piece of equipment that weighed in at 2.2 kilos and hung around the neck on a strap like a dead weight.

We marched for the morning towards the high ground. I was quite enjoying this one. I was stronger and it was nice in a perverted way to know that other people were struggling! The trees cascaded on each side of the path and a clear stream trickled to my left. I thought how nice it would be to come here on holiday and here I was getting paid £100 a month to do this!

Gradually, the ground began to rise steeply and my comforting thoughts began to change. By lunch we were climbing an almost vertical hill. The stream to the left was a gushing waterfall now. We stopped next to a small pool for a drink. The sycamore trees cascaded along the edges framing the water with a gently moving green. I went to the stream and refilled my water bottle. The water was cool and refreshing. Often, when I sat next to water, I thought about my early childhood on the Norfolk Broads. Of catching bream in the rivers and going out on my father's boat.

After bouncing about from children's homes to foster parents until I was 14, I returned to live with my father and his new wife in Norfolk. I was a quiet and somehow lonely child and in my early teens spent more time in the woods smoking cigarettes than in school.

A shout from behind brought me away from my daydreams and back to the rest of the hill. We carried on walking for the rest of the day. Stabia my Italian 'friend' had a bizarre habit that I have yet to see repeated. The insect life in these mountains was fantastic – every bug fly and mosquito found its way into your eyes, up your nose or in your mouth. They were unwanted creatures for most of us but for Stabia it was, as he said, *casse-croûte* – snack-time. He had a great taste for large green grasshoppers. He would always pick up the fat ones about two inches long, rip the legs off the living creature and happily munch and crunch the writhing body. Not being a greedy man, he often offered me a tasty morsel but my appetite always seemed to fade when he asked, so I would close my eyes and dismissively shake my head while waving my hand. One of my French friends told me years later of a shepherd friend of his in the Pyrenees who would herd his stock for days alone in the mountains and live off the land. Apparently, he had lightening hands to catch flies to help sustain him.

We camped in a small mossy copse for the night. We didn't put the tents up but slept on a cushion of wet spongy moss, which soaked us all to the bone. But the next day, as the sun began to warm our cold bones, our clothes would dry just in time for the midday sun to soak them again in sweat.

Three days later we returned to the farm and spent a morning abseiling. Adventure training was over and it was back to camp.

The next two weeks we rehearsed our drill for the 14 July festivities. The French celebrate the day that they had their revolution. It was the day that the Bastille was stormed in Paris in 1789.

We marched slowly in front of the crowd and the mayor. I looked straight ahead but I could feel the eyes upon us. I wondered what they were thinking. Were they bored or in awe? Did they love or hate this crowd of lost souls singing of death and sacrifice? I had never really considered what the French people thought of us. I imagine we were a curiosity. Like a drowning dog or goldfish in a tank. I find it strange how people can be like sheep. Some of us are more like animals than we care to admit. How many times do we slow down to look at an accident on the motorway? Look at how crowds grow; how within minutes we are huddling like cows looking at a dog in a field and before you know it we haven't a single thought of our own.

*

The days had turned to weeks then months. I was soon to finish training and join the regiment that I hoped to go to. The final hurdle was to finish the raid march. This was a 200-kilometre march in four days. It took place in the Pyrenees again. For this one we were divided into groups de combat. All I can remember is sweat and swirling clouds. We marched and marched. When we saw water we would thankfully refill our water bottle; whether it was from a crystal clear stream or a muddy pool. We needed to drink and would drink what we could. When you take civilization back to basics all you are left with is survival. Survival is greed: a starving man would steal even if he believed it was wrong and he knew the consequences. If you are thirsty you need to drink. Like a drug addict mugging old ladies there is very little difference – absolute necessity or the belief of absolute necessity to exist can drive any being back to basics – kill or be killed, steal or die, you or them. The only exceptions I can imagine would be from your own offspring, or on account of religious beliefs – or in our case our true friends.

But we had not gone that far. We would drink the muddy, slimy water because we were thirsty. The march was hard and long and it seemed like it would never end. I had to keep going, I didn't really have a choice: what else could I do – put my hand up and ask teacher for a one-way ticket back to mummy and daddy? My memories helped me – posh girls refusing to give me a lift, champagne drinkers in expensive yachts and the police strip-search in Aubagne. It all helped. It always does. That is how motivation works: anger, abuse, invites to hotels – beat it, and don't forget it all helps. In my youthful state of determination I was motivated to do well. Not to let the side down. Thinking about it I didn't really have a side. My side was my own and I didn't let it down.

Towards the end of the final day we were following a narrow country lane. I was tired – very tired. I had eaten little and drunk even less water. The sun was hot and my body was deteriorating. My mind was wandering. I had my first hallucination. I saw my older brother waiting for me on the side of the road. I was surprised he was there. I wondered how he had found me. I was happy to see him but I wasn't happy when I got closer and he turned into a speed limit sign. But I had finished. Soon I was to start the real stuff that would make the four months of basic training seem like kindergarten.

.... CHAPTER 4

We returned to the administration regiment on the train. We were still not trusted to go anywhere alone, so again we were escorted by the sergeants. I had been in the Legion five months and now I collected the wages owed to me. Five months' hard work for £35! Most of it had gone directly to the *foyer* (the Legion shop) for shorts, trainers and other items. On arrival in Aubagne we stayed in the transit accommodation. We suddenly had rights but we still were not allowed to use them. We could go to the foyer for a beer if we wanted but there was always a corporal giving us a pointless task to prevent us from doing so.

I marched into the colonel's office. I had asked to join the French Foreign Legion Parachute Regiment: the 2eme REP. He looked at me and then at my report. I had a good report. I finished fifth out of the forty men in the platoon. Swartz had finished first and had decided to go to French Guyana as did Rock and Grant. I never saw Rock again. I had heard that you had to finish in the first ten in order to get accepted in the 'REP'. I was hopeful.

'Nine pull-ups? That's not many!' I began to fear the worst. However, I had done really well on the running events and the marching. So he sent me to the REP and I was happy. The pull-ups would come later with age.

Five of us caught the ferry from Marseille to Bastia. As we drove through the town I thought back to the time when I was living on the streets. I looked at the people and wondered about them. I was excited and yet fearful about my future.

We left the port of Marseille in the late afternoon. Once we were out to sea a 1st class legionnaire took us to the stern. I could smell the salt in the air, feel the cold metal of the rail in my hands and hear the crash of the waves against the sides. Every now and then I liked to stop and be aware of myself, feel the air against my cheek, feel the vibrations of music through my body or the rain on my face.

I saw the little green and red badge disappear behind the stern and slowly sink. The 4eme RE was finished. We had thrown our badges that connected us to that regiment overboard, under the orders of the 1st class legionnaire. An old couple was watching as we played out this little ceremony. He explained to them that this was a tradition. We were discarding our original route to become a part of something away from the rest of the Legion. It was ceremonial.

That evening Toureau, Ray, Belge and I went to the bar for a beer. Clinking our glasses we toasted to the future. Belge was grinning from ear to ear. We were moving on. Being allowed to drink a beer on a ferry seemed like a great privilege. However, with only a few francs left from our wages, we had to settle for a couple more before finding a bench to sleep on until morning.

The following morning I was up early and watched the Corsican mountains gradually grow until they disappeared again when we arrived in the port of Bastia. I sat by the window on the coach watching the countryside blur past me. Though the journey was long and slow through the winding country lanes, it passed quickly. There was so much to see. I searched the small streams for fish as we crossed the bridges. Crystal water trickled from the lightly snow-capped peaks into deep dark pools. Once through the green lush mountainous woodland we reached the coastal road, which was narrow and twisting with a sharp drop to the right. I looked at the many wrecked cars that had crashed over the steep hillside towards the sea, rusty brown skeletons painfully clinging to the boulders. I could see rocks beneath the sapphire water and tiny half-naked figures on the beach. This was going to be a beautiful place to live. But I wouldn't be living in it for a long while.

We arrived in Calvi, a small coastal town that I would soon fall in love with. It was a quiet, picturesque place with golden beaches for the summer and cosy family run restaurants for the winter evenings. The town scrambled towards the rock-strewn mountaintops, gradually trickling to scattered lonely houses nestled between the bushes. In the lower quays a sparkling line of brasseries welcomed tourists to relax and listen to the gentle licking of waves against the yachts. Behind the bars, narrow cobbled streets tacked their way through dozens of small shops towards the citadel to the south and the residential areas to the west.

Pictures of the last recorded snowfall in Calvi, which was in the seventies, were presented in the bars like trophies and talked about as fantastic, crazy days with 'I remember that winter. It was formidable. We had never seen snow.' For the first couple of years there would be no snowball fights or happy stories of 'the good old days'. We were just new guys and we were not worth the dirt on a senior's boots. If they spoke, we listened. They were right, we were wrong. We knew nothing and were nothing. We stood to attention outside the 'adjutant's office'. He came and looked at us. We presented ourselves as we were taught in training – rank, name, duration of service and current status (newly posted, which company and section). We each had two heavy bags of our belongings, all of which were exactly the same. There was not a difference between us. We had no civilian clothes or personal effects. We carried our lives around the whole camp to get orientated, which took about an hour. The camp was big but we soon learnt to get to know how big!

We stayed in the accommodation for the men doing the promotion, which was our parachute training. We were the first to arrive, so for the next week we prepared our uniforms, learnt new songs and trained, but in general it was quite tranquil until the others arrived. Each morning we ran with the adjutant who was in charge of the parachute training. He seemed to be exceptional. I looked at his crazy eyes and I was amazed. It was as if the iris was framed with black and the centre bolstered with white. In between the two flashed a brilliant blue. He was scary. I had never seen anything like it and I would never see anything like it again. Later a friend told me that he was the most fearless and professional soldier he had ever met, and that he was gay. I don't know about gay but scary – yes!

We stood outside on the *Zone de Saut* (the Drop Zone). The alternative larger drop zone was situated in Borgo a few miles away. It was late evening and we had managed to find a few minutes to ourselves. Ray and I discussed the camp. It was a perfect location for a regiment that specialized in so many different skills. The encampment was about a thousand metres from the beach and the bay of Calvi, which was 6 kilometres to the south. An amphibious centre nestled between the camp and the sea. It was here that the Third Company – which was amphibious – trained. They had the Zodiac medium sized inflatable boats powered by 40-hp outboard engines stacked three high in the workshops ready for deployment. It was from these that the guys would scuba dive. The more experienced would use rebreathers, a system in which the air you breathe is recycled and enhanced with oxygen. This provides a silent bubbleless dive, resulting in less risk of being seen by the enemy. The only disadvantage was that you could only dive to a depth of seven metres. The Third Company often worked with the French navy and their submarines.

The C130 Hercules aircraft and the C160 Transalls would land 6 kilometres inland at the airport. This was perfect for deploying and parachuting. With the Drop Zone so near and the parachutes being maintained and folded internally in the SEPP (Section d'Entretien et

Pliage de Parachutes or Section for Maintaining and Folding Parachutes) by specially trained legionnaires, we could manage over six static line jumps a day. Beyond the Drop Zone the Corsican mountains towered, with Monte Cinto at 2,710 metres topping the Mediterranean skies. This was the playground for the 2nd Company, which prided itself on its mountain and artic warfare. They had a building – Chalet de Vergio – at which they would train all year round, climbing in the summer and skiing in the winter, a skill originating from the Foreign Legion's battles in Norway during the Second World War. The 2nd Company, unsurprisingly, contained many Austrians, Swiss, Germans and French, having been chosen for their skiing ability. In the winter there was enough snow to ski and the summer offered many challenging climbs. Corsica was a formidable place to train and live.

The others arrived a week later. The four of us – Tremmel, Ray, Belge and myself – were glad for the company.

But then *he* arrived. The man I would grow to hate for many years. Cpl Bleu was a horrible, smarmy, arrogant Frenchman. He had obviously been mistreated in the past; maybe by an Englishman, as he hated us. His whole way of speaking to you made you seethe with anger. He was to take us through our parachute training, which would last three to four weeks, during which we learnt the basics of static line parachuting. Each morning started with a long fast run in the mountains followed by the usual press-ups, pull-ups and the rope. Twice a week we did the 'eight k TAP', which was an

eight-kilometre run with a rucksack weighing 11 kilograms (about 25 lbs), helmet and rifle. It was a fast and
tiring event. Officially, it had to be done in less than 55
minutes, as this was judged to be the longest you could
stay within eight kilometres of a Drop Zone. However,
under 45 minutes was considered a reasonable time.
Fifteen over-arm pull-ups and an ascent and descent of
the six-metre rope in under six seconds using only the
arms were the required tests in order to be accepted to
join a company of the 2eme REP. If a student did not
achieve this, he would stay on for the next promotion
until he could.

Every day for the two weeks we practised our exits
from mock planes made from wood or steel. We dangled
from harnesses and rehearsed procedures for flight and
landing. You could not steer a round parachute very well
so the process was very simple. Our instructor was a
Legion sergeant who would hold his Green Beret
between his finger and thumb to illustrate how the
canopy would move when we pulled the toggles. Once
out of the plane we would check that our canopy was
good and kick our way out of twisted rigging lines if you
had them. Then a good pull on the steering toggles to
steer against the wind, before landing feet together and
rolling accordingly. It all sounds simple.

The day had arrived for my first parachute jump. The
Hercules was not available, therefore I was to jump from
a Puma helicopter at 400 metres altitude. We were quickly
taught how to exit such a small aircraft. The rear of the
helicopter opened up leaving a tight gap from which to
drop. Four of us could jump in one lift. Belge, Tremmel

and Ray joined me for this one. I was excited with my first flight in a helicopter. I was second out behind Ray. We attached our strops to the steel cable. These would pull the parachute from its bag, which was harnessed to our backs. We held the strops behind our arms so as to not get them caught on the exit, causing us to spin.

'Red on!' Deep breath. My heart was racing and my stomach felt hollow. I thought, this is it! I'm finally getting down to business. It seemed surreal. Here I was so far from home in a foreign army about to make my first parachute jump. I could see glimpses of the sea and the beach with the September tourists still sunning themselves.

'Green on!' A horrible siren wailed. I hadn't expected this and suddenly I was clenching my teeth and just wanting to get it over and done with. Ray disappeared and I found myself on the edge of the ramp. Looking straight ahead as taught I waited for the dispatchers, who tapped me on the shoulder, and then silence while the canopy was pulled off my back. I counted:

'Trois cents trente et un, trois cent trente deux, trois cent trente trois, verification de voilure.' 'Three three one, three three two, three three three, check canopy.'

I was surprised by the silence. I had dropped straight down as there wasn't a slipstream from the Puma. The canopy was good. I grabbed the stirrups and did a 360-degree check for other parachutes. I could see Ray slightly lower than me. I looked for the windsock, the smoke or most obviously the movement of the ground below me to find the wind direction, and pulled hard on the handles steering into it. Feet together, knees bent.

Here it came. The ground arrived so quickly I landed in a heap but without injury. It happened so fast. My heart was still beating in my temples. I collected my parachute and ran to the camp only 100 metres away with a huge smile on my face. We shook each others' hands. The French have a thing about shaking hands. Every morning when you met someone you would shake their hand. Not senior ranks – just the people on you own level.

First jump over. The next day we would be jumping from a Hercules. The first jump was cancelled because the wind was faster than the 10 metres a second deemed safe for jumping. The process was almost the same as the Puma but this time we would jump out in groups of eight. We exited from the same side of the aircraft to avoid getting hooked up with someone else jumping from the other side. I was to be number one this time. I stood by the door for the first *sortie*. The first pass was always the *sique*. This was a bright orange dummy with a parachute. This would give an indication of where the wind would take us. The pilot would then adjust accordingly to try to get us in the centre of the Drop Zone. The sergeant beckoned me forward. I stood at the door with hands holding onto each side. This was to help me launch myself as far as possible into the void. I looked down at the tiny figures lying on the beach. I could see the clear ocean and the rocks beneath the surface. At a certain distance out to sea the water became dark blue. I looked up again and saw the mountains in the distance. What a feeling. I felt like nothing else mattered. I felt free, although my life outside on the ground was being totally controlled. Then I heard it; the sound that always spoilt the ride.

'Green on!' And the buzzer. A tap on my shoulder and I was away. This time the ride was rough. Caught in the slipstream I bounced horizontally in the rushing air. The canopy ripped from my back and I oscillated like a pendulum. I went through the drills. There was a long gap before the next jumper came into view. He was Hungarian and although he had jumped from the helicopter he refused to jump from the Hercules. Well, he tried to refuse. Sometimes a man has been strong enough to refuse but generally the sergeants manage to force a refusal from the aircraft. Legionnaires do as they are told – you do not refuse anything!

To qualify for our wings we had to parachute and pull our reserve. The reserve was not spring loaded, so upon exiting the aircraft we had to physically inflate it with exaggerated shaking of its canopy. It would usually catch the wind. Sometimes you would just land tangled in a mess of parachute silk. Either way the landing was rough; usually backwards and almost always on your back as the reserve would lift your legs towards the sky.

We moved on to jumps with equipment. The rucksack was wrapped in a heavy felt liner enclosed by a canvas outer. It had to be rapped up neatly like a Christmas present. On the side of this a further cover held the weapon. We all had to jump with the 7.5-millimetre machine-gun, or the 112-millimeter anti-tank weapon, or a snipers rifle. These weapons always made the exit difficult because of their size and the bulk of the case in which they had to be put. The kit hung from two hooks attached to the parachute. It was released by a single handle Velcroed to the front of the *gaine* (the equipment case). Once the exit had been made and the checks done the kit would be released. It dangled on a six-foot rope beneath the feet. Upon the *atterrissage* (the landing), we would release the kit and gather the parachute with a sweeping motion of the arms. The motion reminded me of small children playing at being airplanes swooping from side to side. The kit was then lifted onto the shoulder and the run back to camp started. We always ran everywhere. To meals, to the stores, we ran anywhere on camp.

We did our final jump and our final physical tests. The next day we paraded outside the block and marched, singing, to the parade square. In most armies when a soldier finishes his training there is a glamorous parade in front of his family. It is more for the family than the soldier. In the Legion there are no families. Your mates – other legionnaires – replace your family. We lined up and sang the regimental song. The colonel and a few other senior ranks presented us with our silver metal wings, which are serial numbered to each man. I stood with my chest out rigid with pride. I had made it to the 2eme REP. I had become a Foreign Legion Paratrooper. It was the hardest thing I had ever done, but life was about to get a whole lot harder!

Later on in the day I went to see one of the colonels, who sent us all to the 1st Company, specializing in anti-tank and urban warfare. I was disappointed as I asked to go to the mountain company. The physical challenges of the mountains enticed me. As with all the companies, the 1st had a sniper platoon and mortar platoon. I was sent to a *combat de localité* (urban warfare) platoon which was quite a new concept and was still a little in its infancy.

The company was away in mainland France preparing for the commando course, which was run by the National Commando Training Centre (Centre National d'Entraînement de Commando – CNEC). The first part of this was run in Collioure, a small town near the Spanish border on the southern coast of France. A Hercules was going to parachute us nearby. On arrival we joined the company, which was housed in an old farm. My platoon was living in one of the barns. We entered to a hive of activity in the late evening and the guys had just come off the ranges. They sat on the edge of camp beds carefully making coffee on blue gas stoves while scraping the carbon off weapon parts.

We were told to present to the sergent-chef. He was a round-faced Frenchman and it was clear that we were for the moment not fit to clean his boots! We were fit enough to clean the seniors' weapons though. An English lad sat down with us and we talked. Ben had been in the platoon three years. It seemed a long time to us *jeune* (young blokes). He said we would be best to shut up and work hard and always stand to attention and present to anyone who had a stripe. In turn we presented to each corporal and sergeant. It would take a while before we would be accepted – first, we had to prove ourselves to the platoon. I discovered that the true selection for the REP happened in the rifle company. It was here where we were assessed. A few of the lads would be gone by Christmas.

The next day we moved to Collioure where there wouldn't be any time for formalities. We travelled in the back of the four-tonne trucks for six hours to reach the camp. I was put in the 2nd groupe de combat led by Corporal-Chef Stein who looked far older than he was. His wrinkly weathered features concealed an experienced 40 years. He had been in the company for 12 years. I would describe a corporal-chef as a floating rank – not a senior NCO and, yet, not a junior. It was a handy rank. He was not under pressure to get promoted and he would go no higher, but he could still serve in a rifle company for many years. On operations and overseas exercises a corporal-chef that was not needed would make up the numbers.

His wages were still good and rose according to the length of time he had served. It was not unusual for a senior corporal-chef to be paid more that a corporal-chef or captain. As a legionnaire I initially earned around 1,250 francs (£125) a month. Within a year I was earning around 6,000 (£600) and towards the end of my contract I cleared around 10,000 (£1,000). However, when we deployed overseas our wages could double. His pension would also be healthy, which took a minimum of 15 years' service with the Legion to qualify. The interesting part is that as well as the final rank achieved counting towards the final sum, the amount of points earnt had an effect – points meant prizes. A soldier would get a certain amount of points for every parachute jump he made, every day he was out on the ground roughing it, every time he was deployed abroad. The more points, the better the pension.

Stein was proud of his family's soldiering history. His father had served in the Second World War with the Waffen-SS. He had his father's number tattooed under his left armpit, which was where the Waffen-SS used to have it tattooed. I imagine it was to help identify the bodies if there was very little left hanging on the torso. I noticed many of the men in the platoon also had their numbers tattooed under the armpit. Stein was a devoted racist, as were many of the guys. If you were black or Arabic then you were not going to get friendly with Stein.

Monday morning. It's half-past five. I'm sitting on a table with Ray and a couple of others, eating a breakfast of a bowl of black coffee with a morsel of stale bread and jam – dipped in the coffee to make it soft. It is still dark outside and there is a thin layer of ice on the puddles:

'I wonder what this is going to be like.'

'I don't know, Ray. I guess we'll just take it as it comes … What are they going to do – send us to the Foreign Legion?'

'Parle Français!'

The sharp voice of Bleu stops our chitchat. I glance across at his pocked face and think, 'Tosser.' We finish off and move back to the accommodation to clean it before walking around the whole area to pick up any discarded cigarette butts and litter under the supervision of the corporals. We are dressed in boots and combat clothing – no berets or belts – and we carry our rucksacks with us everywhere we go. We parade at the top of the hill and are met by one of the instructors, a small fit-looking Frenchman. I don't know what to expect and I still can hardly understand a word of French. He runs off and we follow leaving our sacs à dos behind. Every few minutes we stop to do press-ups and sit-ups. He shows us how to roll forwards, backwards and to the side. When he stops he shouts:

'En garde!'

We stop and put our fists up returning a loud scream and 'en garde!' in return. Our legs are shoulder length apart and our stance is steady. We advance and retreat careful never to allow our legs to cross. This would make us vulnerable and off balance and our opponent could take advantage. We run and forward roll on the hard stone tracks for four hours. Every now and then we stop to learn a new fighting technique.

We learnt how to sneak up on a sentry from behind and break his neck. We were careful to ensure that our heels touched the ground first, rolling forward on our feet as we crept behind our opponent. Once within a few centimetres of my victim I sharply wrapped my right arm around his throat ensuring that I hit his trachea to stop him screaming. I then clenched the inside elbow of my left arm with my right hand, put my left hand behind his head and pulled back. He fell to the ground. In a combat situation we were told to jump back to land on our fronts. The momentum would break our enemy's neck.

We began with no weapons but soon I was carrying a length of rope with which we routinely strangled each other. We learnt how to defend ourselves from punches and kicks while taking advantage of our opponent's weight. We trained on each other, beating each other with relish. There wasn't any wimping out. The corporals made sure of that. Picking us out individually for a sparring session they would punch and fight us with all their strength and we would fight back. This was my first taste of *corps à corps* (unarmed combat).

We didn't shower after the session. We went straight to the stores to collect our harnesses and carabineers. The next half an hour was spent learning how to make a harness out of two nylon slings tied in a manner in which the weight of the body could be supported safely. After lunch we learnt assault course techniques. The assault courses consisted of an assortment of cables, tunnels, bridges, drain pipes and climbs. We started on the *tyrolienne simple* – a single steel cable that stretched from one side of the citadel, which was now the training camp in Collioure, to the other. The instructor demonstrated how to fall off the cable and dangle on the harness before reaching back up and grabbing it with both hands. A strong lift would enable a foot to hook over and a swing would hopefully swing you back on the cable. Swing too hard and you would just end up in the same position as before.

I clipped myself on and laid my chest on the cable. One leg was bent and hooked on to help propel myself along while the other dangled in the void. The head rested low on the opposing side to keep balance. I pulled with both arms and pushed with my leg. It was hard work but the position felt quite stable. I looked down to the waves crashing on the rocks 150 feet below and hoped that, when I let everything go, my homemade harness would hold. All went well and I continued around to the other obstacles. The 20-feet iron gutter firmly attached to the citadel wall was the hardest obstacle to conquer. The trick to getting up was to keep the legs at 90 degrees to the wall to enable as much grip as possible, then to swing from side to side as you ascended. This transferred the weight from one foot to the next, giving that little vital bit of grip. Without this the feet would slide and the body would hang vertically, which meant the arms would work harder and tire quicker and the legs would slip helplessly on the wet wall.

We learnt the obstacles all day. In the evening we went down to the boat stores and inflated the Zodiac boats, which could carry six men all armed with an oar each to get along. We carried them to the beach and unfolded the rubber. Three aluminium boards were held tight with the two metal stays and the air pressure of the inflated dingy. We practised dismantling and recon-structing the boats, followed by an hour of hard paddling from one side of the bay to the next. We finished at about ten o'clock. It had been a long, hard day. I cleaned the toilets, had a shower and went to bed.

'Alert! Alert! Alert!' I wondered what had broken my well-earned sleep. We rushed around, getting dressed; putting on our sacs à dos. Outside in the fresh air I checked my watch. It was about one o'clock in the morning. We ran behind the lieutenant up to the castle at the top of the hill:

'Montrez moi vos quarts!' 'Show me your metal mugs!'

I delved into my bag and searched.

'Down to the sea to fill it up with water.'

'Back to the sea to empty it!' We ran back down the 400-metre hill and up again.

'Show trainers!'

'Show shorts!'

'Show handkerchiefs!'

Our rucksacks had to contain a set list of useless items. Each one was presented but someone was always missing something, so each time we had to run down to the sea and back. This was the Legion's time. The commando instructors had us for the day and the Legion worked us for the night. We finished about four o'clock.

Half-past five – a whistle blast signalled the end of a short sleep. I shaved and cleaned the toilets before my dry bread breakfast. Seven am, and we are running behind the instructor again. We forward roll on the rocks and crawl on our bellies with our hands in our pockets. My heart is pounding as we run the log around the football pitch. We learn how to block an attacker with a knife and how to twist a man's arm and kick him in the head. We beat each other up for four hours. Then we spend the rest of the day doing the assault courses on which we are timed and put under pressure.

I have a supper of lentils and pork. I try to fill up on bread but it's soon digested. After tea we are back to the boat stores. In the big blue we load the boats onto a fast cruiser from which we spend the next two hours throwing the Zodiacs off as the cruiser speeds along. We wait in a small room below deck. The water has made us shiver a little but the darkness is eased with a small red light. A green light appears and the buzzer launches us into a frenzy. We rush up on deck and throw the boats off. Each time we jump after the boats and swim to them and start paddling.

Twelve am, and I gratefully fall asleep. In the bunk above me is another Belgian. He looks very fit. He can hold a biro between his abdominal muscles and he has small scars all over his sides and back. I foolishly ask him what they are from and he tells me to mind my own business. I shut up and later I am glad he didn't get angry. The scars were from training with razor nunchuckers and stars. He was world Thai boxing champion two years running when he was 14. He was the hardest man I would ever meet, and had once broken both of a man's tibias with one kick.

'Alert! Alert! Alert!' I dragged myself out of bed and quickly got dressed. I looked at my watch. I'd had an hour's sleep. We paraded at the top of the hill where Corporal-Chef Stein met us and led us off inland, our sacs à dos causing us to stoop. We march a couple of kilometres to a small bridge where two legionnaires dive under the arch and return with a long ammunition box full of sand, which we take in turns to carry up the mountain. We arrive at the summit as the sun begins to rise. The view is spectacular. To the south lies the calm Mediterranean Sea and to the north the Pyrenees. We march back to the camp and wait half an hour before we become the property of the commando instructors again. We run, forward roll and crawl on our bellies. My whole body aches and my hands are swollen with cuts from the crawling, blisters from the paddling and splinters of steel from the cables. I can hardly clench my fists. We strangle each other for another three hours before we do the assault courses again. We had missed breakfast so I was glad for a bit of lunch. After tea we went back to the boats and paddled for a few hours. Before bed I cleaned the toilets again. It's 12.30 and I lay my head on the pillow; time for a good night's sleep.

'Alert! Alert! Alert!' I just knew it was coming. My heart sinks, I drag my poor, sore body from the bed and we go down to the boats and paddle until 4 am.

It's 04.30. I ask myself if it's it worth sleeping but I'm glad of any rest that I can get. Even half an hour refreshes me. I shave and clean the toilets again. Dry bread, black coffee and back to the crawling and beating. Eleven am, we get on four-tonne trucks and drive to an unknown location. We are near a small river where we spend the rest of the day learning how to make rope bridges. We construct single, double, vertical and three strand rope bridges. We use the techniques learnt on the assault course to cross them. No one is smiling. We are too tired to smile. Our whole lives are a misery and we have eaten very little.

In the late afternoon we are fed. We line up in three groups to have an eating competition between the groups de combat. The last group to finish gets to eat again. I'm third in the line. There is a little egging on but it is under stressed whispers:

'Putain ... hurry up, Bordel!'

I arrive at the front. We are all on our knees with our hands behind our backs and the mud has soaked through to my knees. We are not allowed to touch the food with our hands. We have a whole pallet of sardines to finish that the fishermen had caught the previous night. They are still untouched – nice, cold and fresh – guts and all. The lieutenant dangles the fish to my mouth and I feel like a bird stretching its neck for a worm from its mother. He dangles it far enough so that I can only put the head into my mouth. I bite into it and he pulls away. The guts always stay attached to the head. I can feel them slither down my chin. With the head in my mouth I slurp up the guts like a schoolboy eating spaghetti. It takes a while to crunch up the head. I bite into the heart or stomach. Something fouler than the simple raw flesh and bones from the head sickens me. The taste is disgusting. I have never eaten anything so rotten since. I eventually swallow and I am fed the main body, which is rubbery but not so revolting. The tail takes a bit of chewing to get down. We are lucky in my group. The Spaniard must have lived on raw fish in civilian life. He lifts his head back and practically swallows them whole like a seagull. After a lunch of ten raw sardines I am full and I don't eat sardines for another ten years.

We march along the beach back to the boats and spend the night paddling again and throwing ourselves off the cruiser. We get to bed about two in the morning. The next day is Friday. We do the usual corps a corps. My hands are swollen and stiff and I still have trouble closing them. I face Bleu and shout, 'en garde!' We already hate each other so we fight with all our might. Each time we change roles from attacker to victim. I kick him hard and enjoy the sound of his lost breath. I don't mind getting punched so long as I get my chance to give a little back. We are both tired. My whole body aches and my peripheral vision is blurred with the lack of sleep –

but I am young and fit and my body compensates quickly. I am so keen I don't realize I'm out of breath.

In the afternoon we go up to a mountain. On the top is a derelict building that is a range. We train assaulting the building; climbing through windows and shooting targets. I'm shown how to use a shotgun. I shoot a target a few times when a sparrow lands nearby.

'Quick – shoot it!' I obey the sergeant and the sparrow disappears in a ball of feathers. It reminds me of when I was a young child, about eight years old, when I was fostered to a vicar and his wife. She asks all the kids if they want to go to church. They all say yes, and I think: 'No you don't! You are just saying that because she scares you!' I tell her: 'No I don't!' She looks at me and her eyes do not lie.

Why would I want to go to church? I was eight years old and the world was crystal clear, the flowers smelt strong (have the flowers lost their smell now 25 years later or have I just forgotten how to smell?), and I could run all day. I wanted to climb trees and catch sticklebacks on the marshes. I hadn't reflected on my existence and beliefs, everything was as it should be, so why would I want to go to church and pray for something I didn't understand, worship, without reflecting upon it? I didn't want their beliefs; I wanted to choose my own and one day I would. My foster brother Laurence, who is the same age as me, and my younger brother Pete went to church while I spent a wonderful two hours with my brother Jim shooting sparrows in the garden with his air rifle. The next week and every one after that I was not given the choice over church, and Sundays would never be the same.

I'm enjoying the day because we are not running about too much. It's beginning to get dark but there is one more thing to do before we go back to camp. In one of the buildings there is a trapdoor through which I climb down a rope into the darkness below. As I get to the bottom of the rope, I feel water beneath my feet. I lower myself up to my chest and I am glad to feel solid ground beneath my feet. The trapdoor is shut behind me and I am quite alone in the dark. It is so black that when I put my hand in front of my eyes I cannot see it. The object of the exercise is to find a way out.

I don't know where to look. I feel around with my hands and wade around in the dark. The feeling is eerie. The water is cold and smells of sewage. I find a wall and I feel around the slimy surface for an exit. There are no doors but beneath the water on one wall there is an opening. I don't know where it leads but I have to take my chances. I take a deep breath and plunge under the surface. My lungs are screaming as I half swim, half crawl through the small opening hoping that there is an exit soon. I cannot feel the side of the tunnel and I wonder if I'm going in the right direction or if I'm going to drown in this lost hole. There is no one else around, no supervision or safety staff.

I stand up and my head breaks the surface. I breathe deeply to recover. I feel around a bit more and find another hole, which leads to another room. I can see a light above me. I climb a rope to the top and find myself back outside where I precariously shunt along a steel girder leant against a wall, which leads to a window at the top. I join the rest of my group and we crawl and squeeze through narrow dark tunnels that twist and turn. We eventually come out of the other end and see the rest of the platoon.

On returning to the camp, I clean the toilets again, shower and go to bed. My head has hardly had time to hit the pillow when … 'Alert! Alert! Alert!'

I can't believe my ears. I just feel depressed. Why won't they let us sleep? I'm so tired and stiff. We go out to the boats and paddle in the dark. Three in the morning and I'm so glad to get to bed.

It's 5.30 am and I start the usual routine. I know what to expect – four hours of unarmed combat. We split into groups of six and take it in turns to defend ourselves against five men. Each time one attacks I have to use a technique to defend myself. If he comes with a knife I raise my crossed arms to block, taking control of the hand and twisting it, causing the knife to fall. If he kicks I block and control the leg, swinging him to the floor with a sweeping kick. I finish him off with a punch to the throat. After corps a corps we do our final timed assault courses and the week ends.

It has been the hardest week of my life. I will never forget it. I have been in the Legion six months and finally I am going to get out of the camp and socialize. We don't own any civilian clothes. Even if we did we would not be allowed to wear them, so we go out in combat parade uniform – olive green trousers and tunic with boots. Attached to the chest are my parachute wings, beneath that a triangular badge with a dragon. This is the regiment insignia. Each regiment has a different pattern. On my sleeve is a cloth badge representing the 11th Parachute Division. It has an eagle flying with an anchor over the sea.

I go out with Ben and Ray. Before I can get out I need to pass an inspection. There is very little nightlife in Collioure. We can only go down to a local tavern, which is full of legionnaires laughing and joking while drinking bottles of Heineken. There is another side to Legion life – the social scene. We didn't get out much so when we did we partied! Ray and I are so tired we only last a couple of hours before we are falling asleep on our feet, so we get a taxi back to camp to rest. The next day we are moving to the altitude of Mont Louis to carry on with the course.

Mont Louis lies halfway between the Mediterranean coast and Andorra, about 50 miles from the Spanish border. It is over two thousand metres above sea level and the air is distinctly thinner, but not thin enough to merit acclimatization. We sign out equipment on Sunday night ready for Monday's activities. The first activity is corps a corps again. The difference being that this time instead of rolling around on the rocks we roll around on the frozen ground and wade through the icy rivers. We continue to learn new techniques. I am slightly stronger after a day's rest, so Monday goes well. Each day we do assault courses. They are similar to the ones at Collioure only this time they are much longer and some involve the entire platoon. There is one in which we have to form a pyramid of men starting from five on the bottom to a single man at the top. The others climb over us – using us as a ladder – and, once they are up we tie weapon slings together and haul up the remainder. The obstacles bring the platoon together; new guys stand on the heads of old and bold. We help each other and grow closer. One of the obstacles has an interesting way of getting a man up a wall. Eight men hold a long steel bar about eight metres long upon which I am on the front. As the men walk towards the wall with the pole horizontal I hold on and simply 'walk' up the wall! On one occasion I jump onto a roof covered in snow and slide off, dropping about 12 feet. I land on my back and lose my breath. The small machine-gun I am carrying has hit me in the eye, but that gives me ten minutes to relax in the medical centre while the medic sutures it.

It's late: about one am and my breath freezes as it hits the cold air. The temperature is around minus ten. I'm stood on the icy ledge of the castle wall. To my right is another legionnaire. We are both trussed up in an improvised harness. Between us we hold a long steel bar, and Ray is in a sleeping bag tied with a series of loops to the bar by an 8-millimetre rope. We abseil down into the dark. It's snowing now and I'm thinking this is crazy. My hands are frozen and I have trouble holding the rope. I slip a little and Ray says 'fuck!'

'Stop flapping mate ... just seeing if you're awake!'

'I thought I was fucking going then, boyo!'

I grin and wink at him, pretending that I had purposely done it. We struggle to keep him horizontal and soon his head is sliding towards me. I start to laugh and he says it's not funny! On the ground he calls me a twat and says he's going to get me back for that one. We grin at each other: friends. We're journeying together. It's hard but we're enjoying it.

For a couple of evenings we are taught more survival.

We learn how to make sleeping bags out of old parachutes and are shown different ways of making shelters. One evening, after lessons, we march through the night. We are still carrying our sacs à dos full of useless stuff like running kit and three mess tins. The next day we pitch up in the woods. We start the survival package. Ben is given some flour and yeast so he starts to make bread. I think of the irony. You would have to be stranded for a bloody long time if you need to grow your own wheat and grind flour. But that is not the point. The point is to give us something to eat, as there is very little natural produce in the winter when everything is covered in snow. We are given some live chickens to kill. The instructor shows us how to hang the creature by its legs and put an Opinel knife up its throat and wiggle the blade. I follow his instructions. I had gone ferreting for rabbits and cleaned them myself as a child in the Norfolk Broads so this wasn't a new experience.

The chicken kicked in my hands but it was nice to warm my frozen hands a little on its body. It hung there and clucked for a few seconds before I wiggled the knife in its throat and felt its warm blood drain over my hands. Once bled out, I wringed its neck, covered it in thick claylike mud and popped it in the fire. A couple of hours later we were sat around the fire drinking hot coffee and eating fresh chicken. A few songs were sung before mounting the guard. We had built shelters out of fir branches, taking advantage of a hollow in the ground and covering it with the wood. We were on a steep hill and quite far from a source of water, so we forced a black plastic bag into the wet moss. The water gathered on the plastic and filtered through. Soon a small steady trickle provided the whole platoon with fresh water for the duration. I slept in my improvised sleeping bag made of parachute silk, and enjoyed a cold, freezing, wet night.

Back in the castle at Mont Louis we practised putting mines on moving tanks. I crouched in the hole and waited for the tank to roll over it. I didn't need to jump; I just stood up and planted the magnetic bomb on the undercarriage. To gain confidence with the tank we stood in a press-up position with one arm outstretched. As the rapidly advancing tank gained upon our naked outstretched hands we slapped the moving tracks and rolled to the side. I was worried for my fingers as one of the lads was missing a couple from the last course.

The end of the course was approaching. It was seven am and six inches of snow lay around the citadel. We were about to have our final test in unarmed combat. One of the instructors took me through. I began by crawling through the snow in my light combats before jumping up and running behind him.

'Roulez vers l'avant!'

'Roulez en arrièr!'

'A droite!'

'Plaquage au sol!'

'Forward roll.'

'Backwards roll.'

'To the right.'

'Drop to the floor.'

My heart is already racing and my lungs scream for air. My bare hands are painful from the cold snow and I can hardly move them. Suddenly, someone appears in front of me with a knife. I wrestle him to the floor and punch him in the chest. I am hardly up before I am strangled from behind in a headlock. I start to choke. The drills are second nature by now. I move one leg to one side, lean forwards and grab his leg, pulling it up, forcing my weight to the ground. I hear he is winded when we both fall. I strike with an elbow to the rear and then punch his balls. He releases and I hear Ray swearing. I grin to myself, get up and the instructor beasts me again. I get attacked again and again. The process lasts 20 minutes and it seems like it will never end; but it does, and a few minutes later I am being the attacker for those who had not yet been through. We finish and Stein gives me a swig of brandy from his flask, telling me that the next few days are going to be hard but I would be ok.

We spend the rest of the day doing timed tests on all the obstacle courses before marching into the night. We have three days' food rations and a bottle of water. We finally rest at around four am after building a fire and trying to keep our feet warm in our wet sleeping bags, which we lay upon our ponchos in an attempt to stop the water seeping through. At six o'clock we are on the start line ready for an eight kilometre TAP. After the run we do more assault courses before mounting a four-tonner to begin a march in the hills. The journey is about three hours. I try to sleep but I am at the rear of the wagon, the sides are up, allowing the cold air in and snow to circulate around us. In a half-daze I crouch as small as I can to get warm but within a couple of hours I cannot feel my legs as they are almost frozen. We arrive and march up and down the hills throughout the night, stopping only for a few minutes every few hours to eat some rations. There is no time to make a hot drink as the breaks are too short. We continue to march through the day and into the next night. I'm fit as a fiddle but I feel so drained. My legs are full of lead, the machine struggles but the controller still keeps it going somehow. I am thankful it's cold and not hot. We march into the early hours but I have no idea where I am going ... I just follow the man in front. This makes it worse. You don't know how far you have to go or when you will stop. So you just keep walking. I have had two hours' sleep in three days and I have been doing physical activity without rest. I have never been so tired and will never be that tired again in my life.

Keep walking.

I just want to stop and sleep. I could just sleep anywhere and every little shadowy corner beckons me like a soft bed. But stopping isn't allowed. I think if I had the choice I would have just given up. But there is no choice in the Legion. Giving up is not an option. The motto is 'March or die'. I cannot help but to close my eyes. I open them to find I have walked off the track. Tears well up in my eyes; I cannot believe I can be so tired. Other men have been doing the same for a while now. I can't believe a man can be so tired. I can't see properly. The shadows of the trees are blurred. As we move through the thick bushes each man carefully ensures that the branches he moves don't slap the man behind in the face. It was a simple marching etiquette.

I marched. Everybody feels the same. Some of the

senior guys know a little trick and soon it catches on. The buddy system. We keep on marching, only we sleep. One holds the other in place so that he doesn't stray. He stays awake for a few minutes while the other sleep walks, and this is working! We are still going and yet still getting a little sleep. We do this for another hour before the lieutenant finally decides that he cannot carry his empty rucksack any more and we set up camp. The officer's signaller pulls out both of their rations and makes coffee. I do not want to become a signaller and remember the Morse test that I did in Aubagne. This is a nice, quick stop. I find a place and sleep, thankful that I am not first on guard. I get half an hour before I'm woken again to keep watch. It's seven am and almost light. Two hours sleep has almost refreshed me. It's strange how as soon as the sun rises you automatically feel less tired! We carry on marching for another day before finally arriving back at the citadel to collect our commando badges. And I felt we had really earned them. Le Loup got best student.

That evening we had a meal with our hated instructors. Le Loup is my French friend and has somehow been avoiding the chief instructor during the course. The reason soon becomes apparent as the beer flows and the instructor recognizes Le Loup, who used to be a skin-head:

'Toi! ... Putain! Espèce d'enculé!' 'You! ... Fuck! You arsefucker!'

Le Loup grins and reveals that a few years previously he had beaten up the instructor in a nightclub. We all found this highly amusing. Le Loup was a very aggressive man. He could smoke and drink like nobody I had ever seen and yet every morning get up (sometimes without sleeping) and run everybody to the ground.

He was a stout racist, hating 'coloureds' and Arabs. It wasn't something I agreed with but regardless he was a formidable soldier. Fourteen years later I managed to get his phone number from a still-serving legionnaire and Le Loup was a gentle calm man, matured with age. Le Loup confessed to me at a later date the reason he joined the Legion. He was in a bar fight and had a man in a headlock. Not realizing his own strength, he had heard the guy's neck break. The body went limp in his arms and he quickly made an exit for the Legion. He didn't tell the Legion, just as he convinced the medic when he joined that he was not colour blind. Le Loup was one of my best friends. He may have been a lunatic who had a hobby of beating up coppers on leave but as a friend in the Legion he was infallible. A hundred percent reliable and would die alongside you if that became necessary. We flew back to Calvi and jumped into the camp ready for the next step in my Legion life.

CHAPTER 5

Life initially didn't change much for me when I returned
to Calvi. I moved into my room, which I was sharing with
an Austrian guy who had just joined, a French corporal
who was the room commander and a senior French
legionnaire. I had already presented to everyone within
the platoon but I had not yet bought the traditional case
of beer for my new roommates. In some companies a
case of beer is required for every room. The guys were
happy for the beer but I had just opened a bottle when
Cpl Bleu entered:

'Laisse ça et viens avec moi!' 'Leave that and come
with me!'

I followed him to the showers and toilets where I saw
Ray, Tremmel and Belge. We were put to work cleaning
the toilets and showers for the rest of the evening. We
were the new boys and this was the way they ran it in
this platoon. Each night for the next week we cleaned
the toilets until the early hours. I found this frustrating
and totally pointless. Occasionally, a legionnaire would
pop his head in and offer us a beer, stating disdain for
the Bleu.

Each morning we were up at 05.30, except for Sundays
when we could lie in till 07.30. After breakfast we would

be paraded outside, each man wearing exactly the same dress, which was usually running kit for the morning runs that would last up to an hour and a half around the Corsican hills.

The duty corporal would write out the orders for the next day and these would contain the chores to be done and who was responsible. Of course, I didn't know this, so missed my detailed *corvée* (cleaning job) and was therefore punished and spent every spare minute of the day cleaning the building instead. We were in the camp for a couple of weeks before we started another course, which would last for a month.

Since the 1st Company specializes in anti-tanks and urban warfare, that was our next task. We flew to South Corsica, jumped and marched through the night to the training area. The sniper section had marked the way for us. We were moving tactically when I hit the barrel of my rifle on a large rock and the sound echoed like a rifle shot. I inwardly cringed, feeling stupid and embarrassed. Stein punched me in the head and told me to watch my weapon. I never banged my weapon again and was always careful when moving silently. I was learning fast. Stein was showing me the way. Bonifacio was a purposely converted village for urban warfare. We lived once again in derelict farm buildings. This time we had brought along some chefs to cook the meals, which was unfortunate as we could not supplement our rations from the foyer, so in our hunger we would eat cold tripe or lentils each evening. I read the graffiti on the walls picturing parachute wings, slogans about sleeping with your sister, mother or whore of a girlfriend. We slept on the concrete floors after spending the evenings navigating around the countryside and learning about explosives, which were a large part of the course.

The first few days were spent blowing up anything we could find. We used cutting charges, piercing charges, plastic and TNT that was surplus from the Second World War but was still good and did the job. Stein was still my group commander. He knew his stuff and he didn't care for the rules. A year previously the 1st Company had deployed to Chad and was tasked to track down illegal game hunters. A local hunter was shot by one of the sergeants, and within a few hours the medic decided that he would be unable to save him. The company commander asked for a volunteer to end the hunter's misery. Stein immediately put up his hand, calmly found the man and shot him in the head a few times like he was killing a rabbit with myxomatosis. Later on in the year the company commander and the section commander were jailed but Stein was released after a court hearing because he was obeying orders!

We tested a new grenade for the Famas rifle. It was an anti-tank grenade that fitted to the end of the rifle. You could shoot it up to 100 metres. I thought that was a little too close! It was designed to pierce a small hole through the armour and, due to the inverted shape of the charge, push the explosion into the cabin to incinerate the unfortunate occupants! We fired them one after the other and happily watched flames burst from the turret as the grenade impacted upon the hull. To finish off the tank we cut it in half with cutting charges, put bangalor charges (long pipe-shaped charges designed to blow a hole through barbed wire) in the cannon and improvised 89-millimetre anti-tank rockets to turn it into nothing more than a burning mass of metal. Each time we set off a charge, large lumps of shrapnel would fly over our heads.

The remainder of the time we learnt how to assault the buildings. We worked as three groups controlled by the lieutenant. Each group was tasked to clear a part of the village, which in principle would have been mortared before we entered. We lined up before the first door. We weren't training to rescue hostages, we were training to kill the enemy … collateral damage was not a worry! Grenade in first! The first three men would storm inside after waiting three seconds after the explosion to allow the blast to go down. We didn't want to get hurt by our own weapons. The grenade's fuse took seven seconds. Sometimes, the guys cut the fuse to make it shorter but this was always a risky business, so we would just pull the pin, wait five seconds and then throw it through the door. That would leave whoever was inside less time to react. The first three were in and the targets promptly engaged. The men would then inform the commander what was going on:

'Left is clear.'

'Right is clear.'

'Door on the left, corridor to the front, hole on the right.'

Stein would enter and tell the next three where to go next while the first team covered the area. The same process would carry on until the building was systematically cleared. We trained like this every day using our Famas rifles, which were only 76 centimetres long, therefore easy to get through small spaces. Each building was unique and contained a variety of surprises. It wasn't unusual to enter a room to find the only way into the next was to crawl through a small hole in the wall or to find that a staircase was missing and a bit of a climb was involved. To bring a bit of realism into the training the whole village was practically set alight. Burning cars and tyres littered the streets and the buildings were full of smoke and gas. We trained during the day, at night, with gas masks, without gas masks. Every now and then, to break it up a bit we would go marching for a few days or do some orienteering. We ended the course with an infiltration over two days before assaulting the village. The sergent-chef observed the sentries through binoculars. Each time the sentry turned or looked away we received the signal to move a little closer. The *maquis* (bushes) in Corsica are so thick that in many places it is impossible to move if you are not on a path. We managed to approach unseen before the initial contact was made. We spent a couple of hours clearing the buildings before exiting towards the sea, where 3rd Company was waiting for us with the inflatable eight-man Zodiacs (this time with engines!). We loaded up and sped off into the night. The water had a mild swell, which splashed constantly in my face, and the starlit sky was clear.

As I bounced I reflected on how my life was changing. It was exciting. This is what I had joined for. The hard part was accepting the meaningless trivia. The continuous beastings (physical punishments) and bullshit! Twice a day picking up other people's cigarette butts and the treatment from the corporals. I hated this aspect of the way of life. I was young and I would have to learn that you work your way up from the bottom of the food chain. Eventually, life would change for the better.

The Foch battleship was waiting for some of us. I was in a group that was travelling back by another smaller boat. As we arrived the rear ramp of the boat was lowered. We beached the boats up the ramp and they slid a few metres onto the wet deck. The trick, I discovered later when I was to do this myself, was to arrive as fast as possible and just as you reached the beach or ramp, lift the engine up to avoid damaging it and slowing your momentum. Timing was critical in this manoeuvre. We were transported a couple of hours north back to Calvi where we spent the night cleaning weapons.

The next few weeks up to Christmas I spent working around the camp. We would mount the guard. During the evening there were six legionnaires posted in the shadows around the camp. The stagging (guard periods) were for two hours but, by the time the relief had walked around to each sentry and the required changeover was carried out, it would take up to four hours, which meant I would sometimes be in the same position most of the night. We also had to provide men to do the washing up and to serve in the messes. Although the job was tedious, once the meals were over we would drink all the half-empty bottles of wine and slowly get pissed for the day.

I had washed dishes for a living before when I was 17 years old. I had just returned from working as a waiter on a holiday camp in the Isle of White before I found myself in the Norfolk Broads where I had grown up. I got a job in a café washing up, but soon the cook left and I took over and was cooking sausages to pay my £10-a-week rent on the campsite.

Service week would be very busy as a young legionnaire. One week I had only managed to take my boots off for a period of four hours, as I was continuously stagging on or washing up, which was incredible considering I had not even left the camp.

Kader shared my room, together with two corporals and a 1st class legionnaire called Lepin. During the commando course six weeks earlier Kader had broken his leg and had been in plaster since. Bleu came in for a spot check on our kit. We emptied our sacs à dos and opened our lockers. Kader was a minger. He had not washed his sweaty and by now stinking combats, which were still in his rucksack. Further inspection revealed a collection of toilet paper that he had amassed during incessant masturbation while the company was away. Bleu rifled through my kit but I was fine, taking pride in being organized. The two corporals in charge of our room were away on courses, which left Lepin responsible and to subsequently receive the wrath of Bleu:

'You are the most senior, you are in charge of this room so it is your fault that he is a minger!'

Kader and I stood to attention while Lepin pushed out the press-ups for a few minutes. He was a fit strong lad and after about 80, Bleu became bored, left the room and before slamming the door behind him told Lepin to sort it out.

We stood in silence. Lepin got to his feet, sweat dripping

from his forehead, the veins of his temples visibly throbbing like the one on his large biceps. He turned to Kader and beat him to the floor under a hail of punches before throwing him around the lockers, screaming abuse and calling him the biggest tramp, arsefucker, whorehouse of the world. Once finished he simply turned to Kader and laid down the law of the Legion.

'I have been beasted because of you. You are not suitable for this company. Today is Thursday. By the weekend you had better be gone, you had better desert or I will make your life a living hell.'

Friday night roll-call we stood to attention by our beds, rooms cleaned, blankets neatly folded with sheets rolled up tightly and crossed upon them. Kader was missing but no one was surprised. He would not be seen again. Stein walked in, noticing a small dog that Lepin had found and had decided to keep. Stein stooped down as he walked and casually threw it out of the first floor window as if he was throwing out an unclean boot, demanding what *merdique* (shit) it was.

'We don't keep dogs in the block. Where is Kader?'

'He is missing, corporal-chef.'

'Good.' He left Lepin and I alone, so we had a couple of beers, lit some candles after lights out at half-past ten and bad mouthed Kader. Lepin explained that it takes five years to make a legionnaire and he was going to do exactly that. He had two years to go. He told me about the many people that had deserted and explained that most of them were not suitable, that if you can handle the first year or eighteen months, keep your nose clean and prove yourself to the section then you would be alright.

Around the end of December I returned to the camp from shooting at the ranges a few miles south down the coast. Immediately, I was summoned to see the sergeant-major. People began to ask me what I had done and the whispers started. I had no idea but I smartly marched in expecting to be punched and sent to prison for some benign affair. He looked me up and down and in a low voice asked me my brother's name. I was informed that my older brother Colin was here and that he wanted to see me. Colin was serving in the Royal Artillery Commandos at the time. I was amazed but also very pleased. I was told that if I didn't want him to know I was here then they would say that they had never heard of me or that I was dead. Of course, I went to see him in the security officer's office and that evening, once the weapons were clean, I met him in town.

It was great to see a face from home. I know of men who join and never see anyone from home ever again, settling in France with a new family and at times forgetting a wife and kids back in their own country. We drank Heineken by the port and talked about life back home and the family. My father had been taken ill and my mother lived in Ipswich. My younger brother, Pete, was masquerading as a 'yuppie' in Norwich city – swaggering around with a mobile phone and hanging around wine bars, carrying a briefcase containing his packed lunch – when, in fact, he was a sales assistant in Next!

I introduced Colin to a few French friends and revealed to him the delicacies of garlic buttered snails, brandy roasted king prawns and Pastis with water. In the

'Son des Guitares', a bar frequented by legionnaires most days of the week, I introduced him to a former Royal Marine who claimed to be have been in the SBS (Special Boat Service), the Naval equivalent to the famous Special Air Service (SAS). I doubted his story since we had done some orienteering together and he gasped behind me as we ran. He didn't shake our hands but quickly scampered off to the corner of the bar and kept his distance. Colin seemed to recognize him as being a driver in Arbroath from when he served with the 29 Artillery Commando there. Still, I could never be sure, so the marine lived his little charade and maybe fooled a great deal of people for the next five years. I met Colin for a couple of evenings, but his last night was New Year's Eve and I was, unfortunately, on duty, so I entered the nineties hidden in the shadows outside the sergeants' mess watching an unaware French girl get undressed in her bedroom window.

I spent the next few months jumping and doing exercises in France and in the Corsican mountains, which were steep and harsh, covered in maquis, which create a natural barrier of thorns. Often we found ourselves pushing our sacs à dos in front of us under a canopy of thick bush and spikes.

During one of the exercises in the Pyrenees I witnessed an event in a village, which I would never have seen in the English countryside. An old man came across to my position by the side of a country lane in a village and asked me for my water bottle. He returned it a couple of minutes later filled with red wine, which provided a happy accompaniment to the spicy dried *saussison* and nuts that I had purchased from the foyer to supplement my rations.

A couple of hours later the men from the village gathered together with their rifles and drove off into the hills. They returned in the late afternoon with a wild boar, which they strung up, gutted and divided between each hunter, who would take it back to their families. Wild boar would often come crashing through our positions at night when we worked in the mountains.

During this time I began to get to know some of the others quite well. There was Henri, a Frenchman whose claim to fame was getting sex for a ham sandwich from a homeless girl in Paris, and Pedro, a friendly wiry Spaniard who had spent seven years in the Spanish Foreign Legion. Perez was a boxing champion from Spain and the two Portuguese Special Forces men had changed roles. One who was now a corporal in the Legion was now in charge of his former commanding officer. He would tell me how much fun it was to give him a bit of a hard time every now and then. These Portuguese were fine, fit men. Every spare moment of their day they would be doing press-ups or some type of exercise. It was good to work with these people. I could trust them and we stuck together like mud to feathers. In the evenings – unless it was the end of the month and our wages had run out – we would often gather in a room, get the blue gas stoves and cook up a decent meal, as the food in the Ordinaire was inedible.

In the camp we always trained. After the morning run, the pulls-ups, sit ups and the rope, we would shower, cook some noodles with eggs and do some lessons on the machine-guns or anti-tank weapons. In the afternoons we would sometimes do orienteering around the surrounding hills, and in the evening we would maybe go for a run in our own time or train on the pull-up bars downstairs. Looking back I don't think I could manage to do that much activity now but our bodies could cope and we didn't feel any strain. I used to train with Jean-Louis. He was a friendly Frenchman who had spent some time in a French prison. He would do under arm pull-ups with his legs held horizontal in front of him in sets of five, followed by push-ups and sit-ups. Every night he would be down there for a couple of hours. He told me how, while in prison, the guards eventually wouldn't let him out of his cell as they thought, with his continuous training, he was planning to escape. He was in prison for seven years. I asked him what he had done and he simply answered:

'I broke a mirror.'

I left it at that. There was really nothing more to say.

As my French improved and my wages increased I began to visit the town more frequently. I chatted with the barmaids and locals. Always on the hunt for a little loving! I would go out with Henri, Tremmel and Jean-Louis. Ray didn't go out much at all. He tended to go to the foyer or read a book.

We would not go out without having first eaten the customary *steak-frites,* always accompanied with red wine and then washed down with a few bottles of France's finest 1664 Kronenbourg. Occasionally, we would forget to put a leave pass in to the captain, so officially we were not allowed out after ten pm. After lights out Henri and

I would sneak down the main stairs. We knew where the hole in the fence was to be found. It wasn't the first time we had forgotten to fill out passes.

'Ssshhhh!' We were already quite drunk and tried to muffle our giggles. It's great how after a few drinks you think you are being quiet when, in fact, we had woken the duty sergeant. We had just made it under the fence when we heard the voice shouting behind us:

'Arrêtez! Arrêtez! ... You'll go to prison!'

We laughed and ran for the cover of the bushes before meeting the prearranged taxi to go back to town where we would spend the rest of the night avoiding the military police.

This was my beginning in the world of partying and drinking. It would soon increase to the point where it would be an everyday affair and my consumption rate was something my ex-alcoholic father would not have been proud of! The town was small. There were a couple of discothèques but it was mostly small family-run bars. The 'Son des Guitares' was where the British would generally hang out, drinking and fighting as soldiers do. I tried to have a mixture of friends from all nationalities. I often saw a giant of a man at the bar who would be holding a dwarf who he considered to be his property. Each time he entered the bar he would grab the dwarf and tuck him under his arm like a schoolboy with his swimming stuff. The dwarf would protest initially but he was helpless in the arms of this monster of a man. At the bar it would be 'two bottles of Kro' – always one for the dwarf who would eventually be released in a drunken stupor at the end of the night.

In the summer evenings it was nice to chill outside by the port and watch the girls walk by. I was still very shy with the ladies and inexperienced but the usual port of call was to be found in 'Chez Emile'.

'Chez Emile' was a crazy bar on the port. Inside it was dark and sparkling with little lights around the bar. Emile was a homosexual who would prance around the bar, sometimes in stockings and suspenders, handing out drinks and offering a sniff from his poppers. He was a nice man who would never force his sexuality upon another if they didn't want it. He was also HIV-positive and, sadly, died as I was leaving the Legion. Henri and I would get drunk in his bar and try to count the holes in Annabel's stockings. She was a girl from Paris and was here for one thing only – money. She sold herself for 600 francs for a half-hour and she was never short of customers. A small town like Calvi could not accommodate a thousand drunken legionnaires but Annabel could. She was a nice girl. We would chat and she would never try to coerce you or try for the sales pitch. We knew and it was just a matter of asking. Occasionally, she had a friend who would visit from Marseille, so Henri and I would have a change from counting holes in fishnet stockings and count tassels hanging from breasts instead.

However, it was not always so friendly in Calvi. The Corsican nationalists have an association called the FLNC (Front de Liberation National de Corse – National Freedom Front for Corsica), which is similar to the Irish terrorist organization, the IRA. The FLNC wanted independence from France. Corsica has its own language and history. They are a very dark people with Hispanic features and brown eyes. The FLNC has been known to drive past the Legion camp gates firing from the window of a car towards the guard. On one occasion they blew up a block of buildings near the town. We ran past the next morning to have a look at the carnage.

It was late and my usual crowd were drinking in one of the lesser-known Corsican bars. I had a little too much and went home early, leaving the bar quiet and empty. As the lights were dimmed to close the bar a group of FLNC emerged from the shadows. Henri and Jean-Louis were alone and drunk at the bar. They hadn't a chance. The first baseball bat sent Henri to the floor, unconscious. The second broke Jean-Louis's arm. They were set upon and nicely beaten, then left outside. They were picked up by the Military Police and taken back to camp to be patched up. The next morning the company was ready to take its revenge. Unfortunately, we were so disciplined that when told that we were not to react and that if anybody did they would be severely punished, we let it lie. Reflecting back it may have been the sensible decision, as it would only provoke more aggression and a war between us and the locals. Regardless, being sensible is not always right and it certainly does not always implement justice.

.... CHAPTER 6

It was May, my kit was packed, my arse was still sore from my hepatitis B injection and I was about to make my first trip to Africa. We flew by chartered aircraft in the late evening. As we took off I couldn't help but be excited with my first trip to somewhere exotic. Later in life these trips would become routine, but in the beginning I was excited and on an adventure.

As soon as I left the aircraft the heat was stifling. This was Djibouti in the summer and at 40 percent humidity it was the hottest place I would ever visit. Within a few minutes my clothes were soaked with sweat. We moved to a hanger in the barracks of the 13th Foreign Legion Half Brigade (13 DBLE), which is a regiment consisting of legionnaires of all ranks on an overseas posting of two years.

The 13 DBLE, along with many other French regiments, keeps a presence in East Africa. Djibouti is situated at the only entrance to the Red Sea from the Pacific Ocean and is therefore at a strategic location. From Djibouti, control of maritime traffic can be facilitated. It is also an ideal place for troops to deploy to the Middle East or other parts of Africa.

I collected my kit and immediately started packing for a jump. I had three bottles of water and three days' rations. It was all we were allowed to take, so it would have to last. We moved to the airport and kitted up. Soon with parachutes on our backs, reserve chutes on our fronts and our *gaines* (the harness in which our equipment was packed for parachuting) hanging around our legs, we waddled like ducks to the aircraft. I had never jumped onto desert plains before. The journey was about half an hour, during which the crew passed around bottles of water. I was glad to gulp down as much as I could, as the heat was incredible and stifling. It felt worse as I had only just arrived and I was not yet acclimatized. Sweat poured down my face and I hadn't even started moving yet.

'Red on! ... Green on! ... Go!'

The horrible siren was a relief to hear. All we wanted to do was get out of the aircraft into the fresh air. Sometimes we would sit crammed into a Hercules for hours with all our kit on before a jump. Once the parachute training had finished and you went to jump with the companies of the 2nd REP there was only one way to exit the plane: as fast as possible. The steady, systematic counting of each man out of the side door was history. The dispatchers were sergeants from the Legion and all they could do was rapidly gather the strops as the men exited. A few of the lads had the *cravate* (tie), which was a wide scar across the neck, the result of the strop getting caught around the head – usually the result of not being checked properly. We could empty a plane in seconds. I was to the rear, and literally had to run to keep up. At the door I just launched myself out and held on tight.

Silence and fresh air.

It was suddenly calm again. I could see the other canopies slowly drifting in a line behind me. On the horizon I could make out dark mountains with a hint of red sunrise behind. I saw a mosaic of cracked mud. It was impossible to tell how far away the ground was as large cracks were filled by smaller ones and so on. Without realizing the ground was there I landed. Unprepared, I just slumped to the ground, but the landing was soft. Jumping rounds in that heat was enjoyable because the rising heat would slow the descent, making the landings softer. Some of the older guys taught me a few tricks. If you pulled on all four toggles a few metres before impacting on the ground and then released just as you reached it, the canopy would flare and slow you to the point that you could land standing up. Release too early and you would plummet twice as hard. It was just a matter of timing.

We marched off towards the high ground. Although we tried to avoid the wadis because of the risk of flash floods from the mountains and compromise, it was nigh on impossible. I was sweating and felt weak from the heat. Fortunately we didn't march for long, just far enough to find a place to lie up during the day. We entered a patch of dry, dead reeds, which was the only place to hide. Working on foot in the desert is extremely difficult, but at least we were away from any vehicle roads. The wadis we were patrolling were motorways for locals who were called 'Boo Boos' by the more racist legionnaires.

We set up a guard roster and I soon crawled up in the dirt to sleep. We didn't carry sleeping bags to sleep in. We only took a lightweight shemag (a thin piece of cloth, usually sandy coloured, used to cover the head from the sun and dust) and a desert-coloured canvas. We had to keep the weight down in this environment. If you didn't need it to survive then you left it behind. The sun rose high by noon but I slept like the dead, although sweating continuously. I had already drunk one of my bottles of water. I remembered the saying 'drink little – sweat little'. It contradicts standard procedures in many armies, but the Legion is experienced in desert survival. The system was hard but it worked. The locals drank and ate very little and they carried even less, but they could live for days on end with hardly any water or food. You could live and work on a couple of bottles of water a day if you were disciplined with it. My own mouth was dry and I could taste old socks, as dehydration causes bad breathe.

Night fell like a carpet being rolled out over the desert. One minute it was light, but within 20 minutes it was dark. It always got dark around six pm and light at six in the morning. We packed our gear and marched for a few hours before meeting the rest of the platoon for an attack on a village. The commanders were summoned and briefed. Stein returned to us and drew a map of the camp in the dust:

'Boule de Feu!' 'Fireball!'

It was a little expression that he used.

'Three positions ... we will take the first while the second group – the group of Sergeant Pellier – will take the second. The third group will take the last bunker. On bouge dans dix! We'll move in ten!'

We were to attack the first hut on the right. It was a

simple attack. We were only armed with 5.56 blanks, so it had to be simple. As the sun rose, we approached silently. Someone started firing and the battle started. Each group was split into two fire teams, each commanded by a corporal. We advanced, firing when required, always keeping the enemies' heads down so they were unable to return fire. We never moved unless we had fire coming down from another group. I didn't understand the tactics of it all. I just followed the lead of the corporals, fired my rifle and ran. The local enemy force, the Djiboutian army, keeled over and died. When we fixed our bayonets they ran. Maybe they didn't realize it was just an exercise! We always won the battles. We were always told we would win. Platoon attacks like this are common practice within the Legion.

We filled our bottles from the jerrycans in the vehicles and marched towards Camp Amilakvari where we would stay. We arrived early the next morning in Arta, a small village to the southeast of the capital of Djibouti. Arta was only a few miles away, but we had detoured a bit to add a little distance. It had fantastic views of the mountains and the Red Sea glistening like fish scales to the south. Djibouti, a small country nestling between Ethiopia, Eritrea and Somalia, gained its independence from France in 1977, and was previously known as the French Territory of the Afars and the Issas. It is a strategic location between the Red Sea and the Indian Ocean, and the only possible maritime route between the two. Whoever controlled the entrance controlled the traffic.

*

I found my kit and rested for the day. It was great to have a cold drink, take my boots off and sit in the scorching sun for a little while, but we didn't rest for long. The next day we started to prepare the vehicles for a desert tour. The platoon had an old Dodge wagon from the Second World War, which was really on its way to the scrapyard and three VLRA – *Véhicules Légers de Reconaissance* (Light Reconnaissance Vehicles). They were constructed by ACMAT and were excellent for long trips in the desert. I had bought a camp bed from Calvi town on the advice of the seniors and loaded it on the wagon ready to go.

We set off a day later towards the south. We would tour Ali Sabbih, Dikhil and Yoboki for two weeks. The vehicles could carry plenty of fuel and water, but as we got to the remote areas the water became more scarce and dirty. I looked at it in my mug and saw things swimming around – tiny little bugs that lived in the wells. Still, I didn't have a choice, so I boiled it up and made coffee. We spent the days driving around; however, much of the time was spent towing the Dodge up hills. The mountain terrain was hideous. Tiny little tracks led us through the passes scattered in volcanic rock onto the plains. The plains led us to more hills. We wouldn't see a soul for days and then in the middle of absolutely nowhere we would come across a local family who would stare at us.

These were nomads. They had a hard life but they didn't seem to care. You never miss what you don't have in the first place. On one occasion we saw a family and a small child looked at me with large wide eyes before dashing behind her mother to hide. The girl's feet were dusty and on her shin she had a large open wound. One of the medics cleaned it with Betadine – an iodine anti-septic – and carefully wrapped a dressing around it. They had a tent made from bits of camel skin and old polythene bags, to the side of which the carcass of a camel lay cooking in the hot sun. It was quite fresh – an indication that the family had not been there for long. Once they had used what they could from the camel they would move on to search for the next meal. As we left I looked behind and saw the family examining the bandage with fascinated interest. The girl had a huge smile and waved. I think she was smiling because she had something that the others didn't. She had a bandage. She still had the wound and it wouldn't heal without continuous care.

The first tour was just to get familiar with the vehicles. We returned to Arta for a little rest and once the usual administration was completed we found ourselves with a little time to see the local sights – these were the two bars and the Centre D'Estivage, which was a rest centre for locals and French soldiers alike. I didn't know the village so Ben showed me the ropes. We went to a small bar with a choice of straight whisky or bottles of Heineken. I chose Heineken. A few years later I would have chosen whisky. The bar was small and basic, with whitewashed walls huddled around a couple of small coffee tables. It had one small fridge for the beer. As the night went on the beer became warmer as the fridge got emptier. The locals could not afford much stock so, as the supplies got low, runners would be sent out for more.

These young lads would run around to see the other bar and ask for more stock. This was how it was done in Africa – someone would 'know someone who could', most of the time. I drank. And I drank some more. It was about 2 am and I had had my fill. A young African girl had been hanging around. She wore white robes, as it was a Muslim festival. I had been talking to her – rather, she had been talking to me. She said she was from Ethiopia and just visiting. As I left in a drunken stupor she followed and asked me if I would like to 'faire l'amour'. I hadn't slept with a girl since I had joined the Legion. I just didn't get the time!

I had been on guard in the ammunition compound earlier in the year and had fantasized about sleeping with the black girls in Africa. Maybe this was the time. I asked her how much and she told me. It was about £5. We went to her house, which was a small block building with nothing in it. No television. No phone. No nothing. Just a bed and a lamp. It looked and seemed dirty. I lay on the bed and she straddled me still wearing her white dress. I tried to lift it up and over her head but she refused. She made love to me in a systematic way. In my drunken state I didn't realize she was about six months pregnant. I saw the bulge of her belly under the thin material of the dress, but I was so drunk I didn't even think. Then it dawned on me why she wouldn't remove her dress. It was so obvious. I left and staggered back to camp, disgusted with myself and the whole thing. Coming face to face with a camel on the way, I wondered if camels had morals.

Eight o'clock the next morning we paraded in front of the dusty parade square. Four platoons of 40 men stood with hangovers from the previous night. Some with guilt. Some with shame. Some with a feeling of indifference. Some with a selection of venereal diseases. In a few years I would have that feeling of indifference. A few of the blokes had forgotten to put in their leave passes but, after a couple of beers in the camp, decided to climb over the barbed wire fence for a look in town anyway. Africa is a haven for Legion disciplinary measures. What you cannot do for political reasons in France you can do in Africa. Those to be disciplined paraded in front of the captain in their dress uniform; their white képis immaculate, and their medals shining, with the creases, as always, straight and narrow. They were summoned to the capitan who would decide upon the punishment. They had broken the rules, rebelled ... isn't rebelling fighting and isn't that what we were supposed to do?

During this time in the camp we trained in the mornings and in the afternoons we did sport. It was quite a relaxed time. One afternoon after four o'clock parade Cpl Bleu grabbed a few of us to sort out the drainage. The toilets were blocked. The cause was the full and overflowing underground cistern. We stood in a semi-circle around the concrete slab while he removed it, revealing a steaming rotten mess of toilet paper and everybody's excrement. Bleu disappeared and returned with a couple of buckets and we were put to work. One of the men fetched a metal mug to empty the shit from the hole but Bleu told him to put it away. We scooped our own shit from the hole with our hands and ferried it to the edge of the compound in buckets. A couple of the lads were sick.

I managed to get on bucket duty and this wasn't too unpleasant. I poured it onto the sand between the rocks, closed my eyes and felt a warm but refreshing breeze on my face. I looked across the mountains to the turquoise ocean below. A football shaped island floated in the giant blue pond. It looked fantastic. For a moment I forgot the reality; I thought how great it was to be there. How I was seeing the world and living, experiencing the sensations, the feelings and the fear of the future. I started to daydream about when I would return home to see my brothers. How I would tell them of the things I had been doing and impress them with my stories of the desert.

'Sloane! Arrête de branler les couilles et au boulot!'
'Sloane! Stop wanking and get to work!'

Slapped back into the present, the soft breeze turned back into a foul stench and the afternoon dragged on until tea.

Bleu and his sidekick Collere had been giving the lads a hard time, the advantage of being away in Africa and able to get away with a little more abuse. They both slept with baseball bats by the sides of their beds in case of retribution. They knew they were not liked.

The French had an obsession with volleyball. Most afternoons we would play. I never really enjoyed team sports, preferring to go for a run or do circuits. But Bleu would order me to play and continue to verbally abuse me. I was the youngest and I was English but I was being pushed a little too far. One afternoon Bleu had been sent off the volleyball courts by the lieutenant for giving me too much verbal abuse. I returned to my room to shower, but I was called into Bleu's room. It was going to be the last time. I entered and he told the rest of the men to leave. Their silence confirmed what I expected. We were alone. Angry, I walked up to him and asked what he wanted. He screwed up his pockmarked face and spat his words:

'What are you doing here? Why are you here?'

I didn't know what to answer. It didn't matter. Whatever I said would be wrong. I knew that before I walked into the room that I would have to fight him. This seemed to be the time. I had known that I would fight him one day. It was something that just isn't done in the Legion – hitting a senior rank – but I'd had enough. It was time to end it.

I could feel spittle land on my lips and cheeks. I looked him in the eyes: they did not lie. We hated each other. I decided to make my move. I had never boxed or been trained to fight apart from my unarmed combat in the Legion. I knew he was more experienced, taller, heavier and older, and I knew I would lose. I grabbed his shoulders and went to thrust my knee between his legs. He blocked with his right hand and I grabbed his neck. The satisfying pain in my right fist confirmed a good hit to his left eye. We were close and interlocked. The tiled floor was hard but we felt nothing when we fell – only anger and hatred. We fought for a couple of minutes crashing around the grey lockers. He pulled his head back. I saw it coming but I did nothing: it was one of those moments when time stands still and for a second your mind goes blank. When you break your nose – it doesn't matter how many times you have done it before – the pain shoots to your brain and makes your eyes water. Blood exploded on my face and splattered on my shirt. We stopped eventually, both out of breath, sweating and tired. 'Enough?' he asked. I agreed and we stood up. I left and went to clean up before going back to my room. I walked in and again the room had been emptied. Just four corporals and me.

'En position!'

I dropped down into the press-up position and started to count:

'Un, deux, trois, quatre ... quarante ... cinquante.'

With each press-up I received kicks from all directions. I was fit but when your arms are being kicked you lose your strength. On the floor beneath me my sweat mingled with the blood from my nose. It almost looked pretty, a little like abstract painting or modern art expanding and contracting as my eyes bounced with each press-up inches above it. Sweat stung my eyes and my breath was heavy. I was angry and my arms were shaking uncontrollably. I would get through this. I hated every single one of them. One day, I thought, I would get my revenge ... Patience.

Saved by the whistle: it was teatime. I was released and joined the others in the queue for food. We spoke quietly and a few of the lads thanked me for giving Bleu a black eye and a bloody nose. My hands were shaking with the adrenaline after the fight and the physical exertion of the press-ups. Although my heart was in my stomach as I dreaded the repercussions, I felt good.

After tea I was given a pick and shovel. I could hear the lads laughing and joking in the foyer as I picked and shovelled a hole in the rocks behind it. I finished just in time for the morning reveille. The next morning I went to see the sergent-chef who again punched me in the face, telling me never to hit a senior rank, before sending me back to the others. Bleu calmed down after that. He knew that he had pushed me far enough and that if he continued I would just get stronger and fight him again.

The French navy ferried us across the sapphire millpond to Tadjoura. This was the northern part of the country, which we toured for 20 days. The terrain was open, flat and empty for miles before stretching out to the fantastic mountains in the North. We would pick up any bits of dead wood – it was generally all dead as nothing really lived out there – as we drove, which we would use to cook the combination of fresh food and rations each night while chatting and exchanging stories. It was a nice relaxed atmosphere away from the bullshit of the camp. Even the corporals were being nice to us since my fight. We drank a couple of beers before pulling out a bottle of whisky. A large green preying mantis attracted by the lamps landed on the table. As an uninvited guest we welcomed it with a teaspoon of beer, which it drank within a couple of minutes. Intrigued, we then fed it two teaspoons of whisky and laughed hysterically as it staggered on the table and fell over. If it could speak I'm sure it would have told us jokes!

The vehicles would bog down in soft sand or loose rocks and the Dodge wagon would continuously break down. Ben, also a mechanic, would mend it each time, re-using old parts and adapting anything to do the job. There is a phrase in the Legion: *démerde toi*. It literally means: get yourself out of the shit. It wasn't meant as an insult; it was a way of saying 'improvise'. We would demerde for the next couple of days.

We stopped on the coast adjacent to a steep hill, which seemed out of place as it stood isolated, alienated by the flat desert. For the next couple of days we would have to survive from the land. We still had the vehicles and our kit but we would have to find our own food. I looked around and I could see nothing for miles. The plains stretched as far as the eye could see. Not a tree, shrub or any sign of life. I hadn't any fishing equipment, so with a few others we hunted for crabs on the rocks. This was a start. Snails clung to the stones and we had those too. The sea was rough, and a large wave enveloped me and dragged me out to sea then spat me out like an unwanted fly back onto the coral-covered rocks. I clung to whatever I could and managed to make my way to safety. The razor-sharp coral had scraped my arms and legs. Dribbling with blood, I went to see the medic to get patched up.

While we were scavenging for snails the sergent-chef spent the afternoon trying to shoot the hundreds of scurrying hermit crabs on the beach with a pistol. We found this amusing but there was nothing left to eat from them. He had only shot a couple, as they were small and fast.

We hadn't seen my chef de groupe, Stein all day. It was beginning to get dark and we wondered where he was. A little after dark he returned with a bounty! On his shoulders he carried a huge turtle. He told us there were hundreds a few miles up the coast. We already had snails and crabs boiling. Ben had swum out to sea with a fishing line and a lump of liver he had got from the cookhouse for this purpose. He had left it there for a while before pulling in a shark. Jean-Louis and I took the turtle to the sea, slit its throat and cleaned it up. It was full of eggs, so these also went into the pot. We feasted on shark, turtle and crab for the evening. The turtle was a red meat almost like beef. Survival by the coast would be fine, except there wasn't any fresh water – this we carried with us.

We went further north to the forests of Auday, which was in the mountains. It was the hot season and this was a place in which the 13 DBLE would go to avoid the heat in the summer. It was different to the places that we had previously been. There were trees and monkeys. It was almost green and lush and things could live here.

Djibouti was small but amazing. You could be in the desert one moment, the mountains another and surrounded by running kids in shantytowns the next. As we drove through these towns I was amazed at the children. They ran and played football in bare feet and yet the ground was covered in broken glass. It didn't cut them. Their skin was too tough. The kids would run behind the wagon and some of the men would throw white firelighters with jam spread on them and we would laugh hysterically as the poor recipient would try his best to eat it! Another trick was to tie a bag of sweets to a fishing line and throw it out from the wagon and laugh as the kids tried to catch it! Looking back these were cruel jokes but in my youth and contemporary company it was amusing.

We would stop at these villages and negotiate prices for goats. Fresh food was something we had to get when we could. Half a dozen skinny goats with their legs bound would join us in the wagon and then for supper later. People had different ways of preparing the animal. Generally, we slit their throats; the sergent-chef would kill them with a single punch using his brass knuckle-duster and occasionally, if we had the ammunition, we would just shoot them: but this was considered to be the coward's way out. You had to get bloody in the Legion. This was not a place for the faint-hearted. If you couldn't slit a goat's throat then how would you do it to your fellow man?

We had a fire going and the lads were preparing garlic and onions from the cold boxes. I had a beer and got to work with Jumel, a white Algerian (a *pied noir* or black foot) and an expert in killing and preparing goat. I watched as he demonstrated the way to slice and dice. I held the creature tight between my legs. They were small goats unlike the Billy Goat's Gruff of Europe. Its fur reminded me of a Jack Russell my brother had as a child: we had taught it to seize, which resulted in the poor thing continuously scrapping with other dogs. The goat also had this sort of short hair. I clenched its mouth shut and squeezed tighter with my thighs but it still struggled.

'Sssshhhh ... Ssssshhhh.'

Jumel laughed and told me just to slice its throat. Years later I would walk around supermarkets, bored, looking at people choosing their meat who never knew how it felt to kill their own. I am thankful for my experiences with other cultures. I thank them for bringing reality to my now mundane Internet, credit card, DVD life.

I had my Opinel nice and sharp. It had only a small two-inch blade but that was all I needed. I held it as if I was about to stab someone, with the blade pointing nicely toward my elbow. The goat's skin was tough. A squirt of blood hit the dry dust and rolled, turning into a red worm of sand. With a sawing motion I cut from left to right and yanked the head to the rear. I could hear it gasping for breath as its blood drained over my hands. Its body was still warm as we strung it up by its rear legs to let the blood drain. Jumel collected it in his mess tin:

'It holds much goodness and will be good in the stew.'

I sliced from the throat down to the anus and let its streaming innards drop to the floor. We rummaged around for the liver, kidneys and lungs. Nothing should be wasted in this land. A few locals lurked in the distance hoping for a few morsels. When they saw that we had left the rest of the guts on the floor they arrived and we let them have them. They started a fire on the edge of the camp and waved every now and then, smiling. The meat was stringy and tasted like very tough lamb so we spiced it up with Tabasco sauce. We didn't get a lot from these goats but fresh meat was nice for a change.

We returned to Arta to get cleaned up and see the town. The bars in Djibouti town were dark, and *niahs* (female prostitutes) lurked in every corner. Everywhere we walked we would be offered things: towels, cigarettes or 'hashish' – drugs. We drank. I was with Le Loup and Ray in a small bar upstairs that smelt strange, a smell I would only ever smell in Africa. A few neon lights lit the dark corners. Le Loup was talking to a corporal-chef from the 13 DBLE and the argument became heated, so they went outside. As Le Loup was walking down the steps the corporal-chef pushed him, sending him flat on his face, hitting his mouth on a concrete step. He didn't have a chance to get up before his assailant was on him. I went to help but from nowhere Stein came rushing in, grabbing the assailant, spinning him around and beating him to the ground with a hail of punches. Stein was a hard man and always around if trouble loomed. I respected him enormously. He showed no fear and he was always ready to help. We left the corporal-chef from the 13 DBLE unconscious by the road and moved to the next bar.

I slept with a couple of whores that night. They seemed young. Le Loup slept with three. He said it was an ambition. He would brag to me about sleeping with two English girls in Greece, calling them English bitches.

The next morning we were still drinking in the 'Bon Coin'. We had drunk through the night and the girls were still hanging around at the bar. We met up, exchanged stories of the night's activities. The sergeant major, an Englishman, had been arrested for beating a local policeman. Another Englishman had been shot by a local back in Arta after refusing to leave a local bar. The local, a military man, drew his pistol. At this the legionnaire laughed and said 'go ahead shoot me'. He was shot in the shoulder.

For the next two months the sergeant major would be visited three times a day in the local prison by a legionnaire who would bring him food, as otherwise, in a

Djiboutian civilian prison, you didn't get any. If nobody came to feed you, you would be forced to 'do favours for food'. Stein had told me a story about a couple of legionnaires from the 13 DBLE who deserted and made their way to Ethiopia. They were imprisoned there and sent back six months later, unable to retain their own faeces due to overuse of their anuses. They had to sell themselves to live. I just thought what a couple of idiots!

We returned to Arta. The prison filled up with those that had been caught for jumping the fence after not completing a leave form. If you had a fight or smashed a bar in town there wasn't a punishment. But if you broke a rule in the Legion, if you were late for parade, then the sentence was high. In the sweltering 50 degrees Celsius the small corrugated-tin hut, which could cram 20 sweaty legionnaires on the bare floor, was not a place to go. There wasn't room to move in the oven and the only light came from the small barred window on the door. It resembled an old Anderson shelter from the First World War. The prisoners were only released for a few hours a day to run around the square carrying the traditional half a tractor inner tube filled with sand.

That afternoon we received the familiar:

'Alert! Alert! Alert!'

I had memories of the commando course and my heart sank. But this time it was different. The Gulf War had started. I packed my kit. We were on 30 minutes' notice to move, which meant we were sat on our beds waiting for the call. We waited … and waited. A thought occurred to me that I hadn't really paid attention to before. I may never see my family or brothers again. I had previously not considered this. I was too busy looking after myself and seeking adventure. This adventure could cost me my life. The thought soon passed, and in the future I would get used to saying what could potentially be my last goodbyes. We were stood down. The Paras were not to be used for this one. My time would come eventually.

We spent the last few days of the tour packing our kit and the stores. The Second Company from the REP would replace us. The company was incredibly racist and we were ordered to destroy everything that we left behind so that the 'Boo Boos' could not use it. I ripped up some old t-shirts and towels and burnt them with the rest of the broken camp beds and cheap sunglasses. I was following orders, but it was no excuse.

.... CHAPTER 7

I had been in the Legion for nearly a year and a half but I had yet to have leave. The most time I had had off was 36 hours. Even then we had to be accounted for on the Sunday morning. It was getting to the end of the tour and discussions began to arise about 'La Permission'. Traditionally, we would receive three weeks after a four-month tour. We had been saving a reasonable amount for this, as our wages when we were abroad would nearly double. Of course, I had very little to spend it on. I had bought a Walkman, some cassettes and a few other bits and bobs but, generally, I spent my money on food and drink. It was rare that I didn't go out without having a good meal in a local restaurant. Djibouti town was an exception. The food was generally pretty bad and rotten unless you knew where to go, which we didn't.

We flew back on a Thursday. I looked out of the window as we descended to Bastia. Everything was so green and lush in the warm September afternoon compared to Djibouti. We were all smiling and joking as we unloaded the kit and cleaned it. We were excited at the prospect of a little time off and, hopefully, an encounter with a French girl or two. Friday evening I went with Le Loup to book a flight to Paris. We had only been given a week's leave because we had to return for the Fête de St Michel. I had handed my passport to the guard commander when I joined in Aubagne and I had not seen it since, so I decided to stay in France with Le Loup. I had saved 20,000 francs (about £2,000) and I intended to spend the lot in a week. We bought some civilian clothes; a pair of jeans and a denim shirt and hid them in a bag. I would have to wear my parade shoes until I could buy a new pair. We were still not allowed to own civilian clothing, but once we were away from the Legion and we were properly on leave we would once again be entitled to put them on.

Saturday afternoon. The rooms had been inspected and we rushed to the gate with huge grins on our faces. I hadn't felt this way since I was a young child breaking up for the summer school holidays. We jumped in a taxi and went directly to the town to start the party. Our flight wasn't until 7 pm, so we had time for a few beers and to say hello and goodbye to the local barmaids. We laughed and joked. I was excited with the prospect of seeing Paris and we were determined not to waste a single minute of our time off, so we took taxis everywhere. There was no time to waste. We had to live the fastest week of our lives. We didn't know when we would get another chance, if ever. It could be another year and a half or longer.

From the five-star hotel, Le Loup took us straight to a nightclub he knew. 'La Scala' was a three-story club owned by a former legionnaire. A queue snaked down the Rue de Rivoli.

'Ne vous inquiétez pas les gars!' 'Don't worry lads!'

We went straight to the front and the doorman stepped outside to clear a space. I felt like a celebrity. The owner knew that the legionnaires would be good customers, spending their savings like there was no tomorrow. We ordered a couple of bottles of whisky and propped up the bar all night. More legionnaires began to turn up. I looked around and saw an array of attires being worn: parade trousers with a civilian shirt, army boots and jeans with an army jumper. Not everybody had had the chance to buy some clothes, so wore whatever they had. We didn't care. We were the worst dressed men around. We had no time for fashion and we certainly didn't care what our hair looked like. We cared about drinking and sex. Nothing else.

I had travelled all the way to Paris but I did not move from the bar. The most I saw of the city were the steps to the bar and the toilets. Drink. Drink. Drink. We were at the bar when it suddenly dawned on me that girls were just hanging around us. It hadn't entered my mind to try to pull a bird. The lads would have to wait as I focused on Marie. I leant forward, and touched her waist, to hear her over the loud music. She smelt clean and of perfume, which was strangely alien to me now, but somehow comforting. She had inherited a large amount of money from her father who had been a fighter pilot in the French Air Force and had died in a crash. We drank until dawn, when I took her out for breakfast before meeting the rest of the lads at the hotel. Le Loup was there, completely wasted, eating his napkins by mistake, instead of his croissants. The couple on the table next to us tried to avoid eye contact, clearly embarrassed and intimidated. We paid the bill, collected our bags and went to the Gare de Lyon with our matching green para-bags slung over our shoulders.

We had an hour to wait for our train, so we ordered croissants and litres of beer. I spoke to Le Loup in a mixture of French and English. He enjoyed speaking English every now and then. My French was now quite good. My accent had almost gone. I spoke like Le Loup and the others. It was a rough, street French. Slang and swearing made up most of my dialogue. My foul language would embarrass most people. Years later I was in a French conversation class with the British army. The discussion became heated and the tutor stopped the conversation, telling me that I was embar-rassing her with my language! I didn't think it was bad. It was just the way I had learnt to speak. I learnt to speak like a child again; mimicking words and phrases but never truly understanding how each sentence was formed. The more courses that I did, and the more expe-rience I gained, the better my knowledge and vocabulary became. Le Loup taught me some *verlan*. This was a type of Parisian slang. I can only liken it to cockney rhyming slang. The words were inverted to form a strangely familiar but foreign French: 'Je vais te taper un coup de tronche' ('I'm going to give you a head-butt'), became 'Je vais te *perta* un coupe de chetron'.

While seated in Gare de Lyon café, someone suggested we put our uniforms on for the train journey, to avoid getting trouble from the conductor. This sounded a good idea and proved to be sage. So, a few minutes later we had stripped from our civilian clothes down to our

underpants, continued our breakfast of beer and croissants, putting our uniforms on just before we left to
board the train.

My English accent had begun to change. I spoke less
and less English. I now sounded strangely foreign. An
English lady approached me, commenting on how good
my English was! I thanked her and explained that is was
due to my being English in the first place. She had
believed that I was French!

We hadn't slept yet. We spent the six-hour train
journey in the small bar, which had to be replenished on
one of the halfway stops. The pretty serveuse chatted to
us as we slowly began to drink the bar dry. The
conductor arrived and, upon seeing our joviality and
uniforms, joined us in a drink. He didn't finish his
rounds, choosing instead to stay with us. After a dozen
bottles of Heineken, we persuaded him to leave the train
at Chambéry – where Le Loup was stationed with the
French Alpine Commandos – to join us for a drink in
town. Eventually, we were so drunk that we all got separated and had to find each other later. It wasn't difficult
as the town was small. I asked if anyone had seen any
other legionnaires and I was soon put in the right direction. I don't know what happened that afternoon, I was
simply too drunk to remember. One of the lads woke up
in the middle of a road a few miles from the town with no
idea where he was or how he had arrived there.

I found Le Loup. He was eating raw mince on a park
bench. 'Steak Tartare' he called it. It was normally a French
delicacy served on a plate with a raw egg in the middle,
but he was happy to eat it straight from the butcher's

bag. I shared it with him before we looked for a hotel. That evening I met some of his friends, who agreed that he was completely barking mad. We drank and went to a club for whisky later. My body just could not take any more punishment, so I left around midnight to get some rest.

Seven o'clock. Le Loup bursts in, dressed for a run, waking me from a dreamless sleep. I got dressed and off we went for a good hour to clean out our systems. After a good sweating session and a shower I felt that I had fully recovered. We spent the Monday morning looking for more clothes and chatting to the many pretty shop assistants, arranging to meet later. A couple of girls joined us and we chatted about nothing for a couple of hours. That evening I was to get too drunk. We started in the local bar. Le Loup's friends arrived and the drinking games started. A few hours later I had finally managed the art of drinking a glass of beer without it really touching my mouth. With a little practice I could open my throat and just pour it in! I went upstairs feeling a little sick. Suddenly, without warning, my body exploded. Projectile vomit sprayed the walls of the toilet and it kept on coming. It was disgustingly incredible but I soon felt a lot better and promptly went back to the stairs before deciding that it was time to slide along a table like they do in old western films.

A group of Italian tourists were not too happy that I had chosen their table for the feat, but I sent a round over afterwards. Hanging from the banister with one hand I let myself go and managed to spill every glass on the table, almost knocking out one of the tourists before promptly making my way back to the bar where the concerned barman put his hand on my arm and asked me if I was ok. After vomiting on his hand I told him I was fine and carried on with the party. It wasn't long before a couple of lads bundled me into a taxi and carried me back to my room.

Seven o'clock and Le Loup was back again. Off we went for another good hour. The same receptionist was still on duty from the night before. She had seen me being carried in in the early hours of the morning and looked stunned to see me get up and go for a run. I don't think my body ever recovered that quickly again. But youth is a good healer and our bodies can withstand a lot of abuse.

On Thursday I returned to Paris to meet Marie. I found a hotel and went back to La Scala. I had arranged to meet her there but when I telephoned at midnight to see where she was she was still in bed. The French don't socialize like the English. There is very little point in going out before midnight because the bars will be quiet till then. People really started to arrive around three or four in the morning in La Scala. I met Marie and bought her a whisky and coke. We talked for a while but after a few drinks she seemed to be distracted. Her friend arrived and advised me not to let her drink any more. I felt this was strange but I didn't take any notice.

Every half an hour she would disappear for a few minutes. This happened a few times. So I decided to follow her. She had a lovely figure, just visible through her little red dress. Parisian women have a way of moving that would always capture the imagination. From a distance, I watched her visit every single bar in the club. It was getting late, almost seven am, and the dance floors were beginning to empty. At each bar she collected all of the remains from all the glasses, poured them into a single glass and then drank the lot. I followed her. It was her last tour but she must have done the six bars in the club quite a few times during the evening. I sat with her at a table and I tried to speak to her for a few minutes before she slumped on the bench. I was unable to wake her so I left her there, trembling with alcohol, got into a taxi and picked up a prostitute in Rue St Denis who gave me oral sex in the back. I began to wonder if there was any point in trying to date in the Legion. Women didn't want to go out with somebody they would never see again. I found that prostitutes were guaranteed and cheaper. A lot less hassle and I didn't have to chase. But I still chased anyway. It wasn't sex that I needed. It was compassion.

I returned to Chambéry. We continued to party through the weekend. Each morning we went to the café by the railway station because it opened early. We could finish in the club and carry on drinking there. Our last night was Saturday. Throughout the week we had met a few people. We were a bit of a novelty because legionnaires were very rare in the town. The young girl that had been hanging around us all week was still tagging along like a lost puppy, having slept with almost all of us. She was slim and short, but she smoked continually and swore like a trooper.

I tried to pay at the club entrance every night but they refused to take my money. The last night was great and yet also sad. We knew that this different life that we had experienced – this freedom to do as we pleased, to be ourselves – would end and we would soon be going back to the Legion. The Legion was a hard life but somehow I was always glad to get back. I knew exactly what my life was in the Legion. I knew where I stood in relation to things. Outside on leave I had no purpose. I had no reason to do anything. My only mission was to get drunk and get laid. That last evening the locals had bought us bottles of champagne and whisky. They were lined up on the bar. There must have been at least ten. This gesture was warming. We were respected for being in the Legion.

However, I didn't understand the reasoning behind this respect: we were all ultimately in the Legion through choice. Our initial motivation was purely self-interested. We didn't join for a desire to serve France: we joined because we just had to or wanted to do something different with our lives. Once inside our only loyalty lay with our friends and to the Legion. We were totally devoted to die for France, but only because France owned the Legion. France had a great tool: an army of foreigners – disposable and yet politically great for the voters as apart from the officers, nobody in the Legion was officially French. Any Frenchmen in the Legion were renamed and became Swiss, Canadian French or Belgium – well at least according to their military identity cards.

We flew back on Sunday evening. A few faces, mainly the older French corporals, were surprised to see me back, thinking that I would desert. We exchanged stories of our leave with the remaining lads. I was glad to be back, knowing that we would soon receive a new intake and at 19 years old I was hoping to be replaced as the youngest man in the company. I was hoping somebody else could take my nickname of *gironne* (baby face). The Fête de St Michel had returned once more. A week of challenges lay ahead: the companies would compete against each other. It would end in a parade, presentations and a huge party for a couple of days.

Monday morning. Over ten men had not returned and never would. I had hardly eaten the previous week. At around 7.30 am, 800 of us huddled together at the airport. We were all dressed in boots, combat uniforms, helmets and Famas, with a 12-kilogram rucksack on our backs. The eight-kilometre race was about to start. Individual and company prizes were to be won. The colonel stood 50 metres to the front. He brought us to attention and shouted:

'En avant!'

Off he ran, his rucksack bouncing up and down giving the impression that he was bobbing his head up and down. We set off and the ground trembled. Hundreds of heavy stomping feet stirred the dust. It rose and obscured our view. We started at a sprint but soon we were screaming for breath. At the end of the runway the path was narrow and could only fit a Land Rover. The trick was to get there first. Then you had a head start. Arrive later and you would have to fight your way to the front and get slowed down. After finishing leave I had returned more determined than ever. Bleu was up at the front. I stared at his back with hatred. I would beat him. I dug in. Dig deeper. Come on! Catch the bastard. I egged myself on. My shins burned and my legs began to feel tight. It was halfway and the group had begun to thin. There was room to overtake so I pushed a little harder. I saw Bleu on my left. I looked to my memories for motivation: bucketing shit in the desert, a broken nose and the fight, digging holes in the desert. It all helped to keep me angry and strong, and in a way it did me good. I didn't look as I passed him, knowing that he would see me go by. Done it!

I knew he had seen and there was no way he was going to catch me up now. I pushed harder. Keep going. Keep going. White tape channelled us to the finish line. I stopped at the chronometer and wretched some green bile on the back of the leg of the man in front. He didn't notice, as he was too busy gasping for breath like the rest of us. It was a frothy liquid substance, as my stomach was empty. I had finished well. Thirty-five minutes and eight kilometres of pure anger. Bleu arrived two minutes later and I enjoyed the satisfaction. Sometimes it's good to get revenge in a subtle way. He leant forward with his hands on his knees, staring at me. I was getting stronger and he knew it. And it felt good.

We showered and prepared for parachuting. The competition was to find the fastest combat group to parachute, pack our kit and run back to the camp. The stopwatch started when the green buzzer frightened the life out of you. We jumped. I was to the rear just in front of Stein. I landed, rolled, quickly unclipped my kit and wrapped my parachute around my arms before heaving my kit onto my back. Once again I was running with all my might but I was weaker from the eight-kilometre TAP. We arrived at the finish but Stein was missing. All eyes were to the sky. I could see a figure bouncing to the rear of the Hercules. It was Stein still hooked by his strop to the aircraft.

'Look at that crazy German bastard … that bloke is fucking nuts!'

I nodded to Le Loup to show my agreement. They were all nuts, I thought.

Six men pulled him back in slowly. On the ground he revealed that he had unhooked his strop, sneakily tying it to his harness for a laugh. The Legion dispatchers were in on the joke. It was a crazy, brave thing to do but he laughed it off and spent a couple of weeks in prison for his trouble.

The next day we did the assault course as a group and finished with a fitness test. We each had been given a task. I had to do as many sit-ups as possible in a minute. The others had to do press-ups and pull-ups. There are some incredibly strong, fit men in the 2eme REP. I was to witness this. Stowski was a 1st class legionnaire in the Fourth Company. He was a short stocky man and looked like he would be at home as an Olympic gymnast. He jumped up and did 56 over-arm pull-ups in a minute. We stood impressed but his group was a man short so somebody had to go again. He jumped up and did a further 45!

St Michel was over. For the next few months we continued with the exercises and training. I went out most evenings I had the chance. Ray started to freefall parachute at the weekend and I joined the pistol-shooting club. I learnt to drive – badly – and fold parachutes. This was a horrible thing to do. Two weeks of trying to force silk into bags that just seemed too small, neatly packing the parachute cord with elastic bands. It was boring but most people learnt it: it was done to enable us to do more parachute jumps. We were independent of the French army and self-contained. All we needed was a pilot and a Hercules and we were away.

It amazed me meeting some of the blokes. Hank was a softly spoken and very quiet, tall, slim American. He wasn't aggressive, which was unusual but also recognized, so soon he was working for the service company as a clerk. We got on ok simply because of our common tongue. He spent a year with the rifle company before getting a desk job to take life easy, while I was always keen and looking for new challenges. He was a scientist back home with a wife and child. He showed me a photograph of an overweight family on holiday. I wondered why he had left it all at 34 years old. Maybe he just thought he had to go and do it before he was too old.

It was during the parachute-folding course that the 2nd Company flew to Chad for operations. I was furious. We were the lead company but we had stayed behind. They were to evacuate the French nationals. This was often the case in Africa and the 2eme REP were usually deployed to do this at least once a year. We were always on eight hours' notice to move, which was the reason for the evening roll-calls and leave passes. We were only allowed to visit Calvi in the evenings so we were easily recalled. A few days later I decided to ask for a posting. I thought that if I wasn't going to deploy with the 1st Company, then I would cut down the Guyanese jungle of French Guyana for a couple of years. Thinking back I should have been patient, but at the time I was keen but disappointed. I was told that there weren't any places in French Guyana so I accepted a posting to the 13th Half Brigade back in Djibouti.

.... CHAPTER 8

I was due to leave for the 13 DBLE in May 1991. I was given three weeks' leave beforehand to say a few hellos and goodbyes. This time I went home. I managed to catch the ferry and I was allowed back into the country using my French army identity card. I knew my younger brother had moved to Cambridge so I went there first to track him down. He was living in a flat in the city. As the taxi arrived I saw him walking along the street, so I waved frantically. His startled expression surprised me. It was not directed at his brother arriving on the side of the road but at the unknown shaven-headed tanned thug waving at him. A few seconds later and he suddenly realized who I was! Amazed, we greeted each other and promptly went to his flat and chatted while he made spaghetti bolognaise. I had changed into a fit and confident man, hardly resembling the boy that had joined the Legion almost two years previously. My outlook on life was different. He was more concerned with making money and following the labels of fashion, whereas I sought life experience and something different. I realized I would probably never really know him again regardless that we had grown up together. We were different now. We needed different things in our lives and we had different opinions. He would always be my brother but we were no longer children and as adults we had almost become strangers.

We visited the local bars and clubs. I was keen to chat to the girls after a few beers and my fit tanned looks attracted a little attention, but I found the truth pushed them into a disbelieving, cold attitude. I hadn't realized that telling people I was in the Foreign Legion could result in such a reaction. They were not in awe and I didn't want them to be. They simply would not believe me and if they did, then who wants to go out with a man that is going away for two years? So I moved into lying and telling the ladies that I was a bricklayer who had just returned from holiday in France. This was far more acceptable, so I was soon considered to be 'normal' and not some lying young lad fabricating stories to impress the ladies. I visited my other brother and my mother for a few days but I returned to Paris to meet a girl I had met and to see some friends.

I had to catch the ferry from Corsica to France to join the 1st Foreign Legion Regiment. From there I flew from Paris and back to Djibouti. I would not return for two years. I was to join the 3rd Combat Company, where I met a few other friends from the 2eme REP who were also posted.

An English sergent-chef, who was formerly an officer in the Royal Marines and an excellent soldier, ran the sniper platoon. I felt that there was something different about this place. People were friendlier and there seemed to be less stress. There wasn't an evening roll-call so we could go to town without having leave passes. It was a welcome change from the discipline of the 2eme REP.

In the REP, I had been taught to believe that we were a cut above the rest of the Legion but I soon realized that there were also excellent soldiers in the 13th. Most of these good men returned to France after their two years to become paratroopers themselves. I had barely unpacked my things when I found myself driven to CECAP (Centre Commando d'Arta Plage). This was the commando-training centre based at Arta Beach, 21 kilometres down a single dusty track from the main village. I had been here a year previously to do the assault courses and some boat work.

I joined my new section. To my surprise I was to acclimatize and not be involved in the course. This seemed very unusual to me. For the first time in my Legion career I wasn't going to be beasted. However, within a couple of days the course was cancelled and we were deployed for Opération Godoria. This was on the Ethiopian border, where civil war had broken out. The refugees, the army and the rebels were all fleeing into Djibouti and other neighbouring countries. We drove for a few hours to reach the border. I was sitting next to a guy from East Germany. Vilder had narrow bright blue eyes and a strange rounded back, yet he stood proud. He had just finished the promotion course for corporal but had not yet been promoted. This was an aggressive and extremely fit man. His mannerisms and eyes revealed a deep-set hatred for anyone who was not in the Legion. The rest of the world was dirt under his feet.

We arrived at the border. Hundreds of people

surrounded the vehicle. I wasn't sure what our role was as we had not been briefed, we were told just to get there and sort it out. On arrival Vilder immediately jumped from the wagon and began to beat anyone that came into his vision with the butt of his sniper rifle. He was a strong man and very few people got up from the floor after he had hit them. A captain came running over waving his arms frantically. He was visibly distressed.

'Arrêtez! Arrêtez! We are here to help them.'

'Oh!'

Vilder, clearly disappointed, collected his day sack and walked off to see if there was anyone who didn't need help. Humanitarian aid wasn't really the job legionnaires wanted but there was no choice in the matter. There was a tailback of a few kilometres on the border. A couple of local border guards could not handle this influx of refugees, who were absolutely not allowed to enter. So we set up a barbed wire fence and channelled them through. Army and rebels alike were searched and their weapons and vehicles taken from them. The piles of AK 47s and Duchcas 12.7-millimetre anti-vehicle/tank/ aircraft automatic machine-guns (Russian versions of the American .50-calibre Browning, which we used within the Legion) rose to about 20 feet. A couple of bits and bobs soon found their way into the pockets of a few brave legionnaires. The soldiers and civilians were loaded into wagons and promptly driven to another border where they were deposited back in Ethiopia! This was Africa. Djibouti had enough problems of its own without Ethiopia.

We spent the next few days organizing a bit of food and

water but not before we drove over the border to have a look around. We found a few weapons and grenades, so we had a little shoot and threw a few grenades about. But generally there didn't seem to be much of a threat, so we returned to sort out a little humanitarian aid. Médecins Sans Frontières arrived and helped with the medical matters alongside our own medics. The problem was the lack of water. These people had not drunk for a few days. We organized a barbed-wired funnel to a water supply. This was controlled with lines of legionnaires pushing back the crowds with our rifles:

'Reculez! Reculez!'

They soon began to mimic us, which we found annoying. If they didn't want to drink, we thought, then we may as well go home.

We allowed women and children to come to the water first. They arrived with empty paint cans or bottles and filled up. People were clearly dying of thirst. We had already found a few corpses of old men and small children among the crowds of thousands. It's back to basics, back to survival. When it comes to the bare necessities of life we all become selfish. I moved forward, took the water off a woman washing her feet and gave the old man a drink. Eventually, the crowds died down and left. We stayed behind to clean up the mess before returning to camp to reconfigure for the next task.

The weekends in Djibouti are on Thursday and Friday. One Thursday we met in the 'Bon Coin' for a platoon party. Mac had just joined the platoon from the REP. He was a short stocky lad from the north with an array of tattoos. He had joined the Legion in a bizarre manner.

His friend had beaten his girlfriend with a hammer. Thinking that he had killed her he asked Mac to accompany him to the Legion. Mac agreed and went through the joining process to keep him company without the intention of actually staying. His friend wasn't accepted but Mac was and just decided to stay anyway!

We became good friends and soon had a reputation in the company for going mad in the town. We were heavy drinkers and caused havoc in the local bars. The Platoon visited a local Ethiopian restaurant, which was dark and smelt strongly of frankincense. Wot, an Ethiopian dish, was a pancake served with an unknown meat. We sat cross-legged as the girls came around us and fed us with their hands. Not only did we get to eat what tasted like rotten dog, but we also had dirty fingers shoved down our throats. A few of us went down the small side alleys looking for bars. People lay around on the dusty dry mud roads and we were continuously approached:

'Serviette? Serviette?' 'Towel? Towel?'

'No, fuck off!'

'Quoi Fucking! Quoi Fucking!'

'Stop fucking following me ... I don't want a fucking towel. I'm on the piss not on the fucking beach ... Fuck OFF!'

'Cigarette? Cigarette?'

'No! I don't want a Cigarette either ... Do you want a Fucking Punch ... hampsheek, hampsheek!'

We taught ourselves a few local words for blow job (*goulou goulou*) and bugger off (*hampsheek*). In return we learnt from the locals how to ask for money (*baksheesh*), but often they would just look at us and hold out their hands. For the first few weeks I could tolerate it and gave a few things away, but after a few months and eventually two years I would have little patience. I didn't think about these people only trying to survive. I didn't appreciate that: I just wanted them to leave me alone.

Occasionally, we saw a local empty his bowels on the pavement. The whole place stank. So we drank and went nuts. In one of the small bars we began to dance on the tables, which quickly turned into firewood. I went to the rear room to find the toilet. But the door was locked. Jacque was a *pied noir*. Seeing my dilemma he helped me smash a large hole through the door just to discover a broom cupboard. Disappointed, we went outside to piss on the streets like everybody else.

Mac and I started a competition and soon began the biggest breast contest in the bars. Young girls would queue up and show us their prizes in the hope of being the winner. There wasn't a prize except the possibility of getting 5,000 Djiboutian francs off us later when we were a little more drunk. We met up in the 'Bon Coin' the next morning. I picked up a lightly built hooker and went back to a cupboard under the stairs. There was just enough room for a mattress. I was terribly drunk and she laughed hysterically, looking at me with her legs wide open, lying on her back. She was clearly insane. She laughed some more and pulled off her knickers to reveal a mutilated vagina. Some of the local girls are sutured with camel hair when they are young. They also are circumcised and at times the whole labia is removed, leaving a gaping hole. Her vagina looked like a zip where she had removed the camel hair when she came of age, so that she could go on the game. I left her there demanding money for what I could not do, and returned to the Bon Coin to join the rest. I was rapidly going off the prostitutes.

Djibouti offered very little for a young man in his early twenties. There were very few French girls. If we heard that there was one in town we would search the bars to try to find her. On one occasion we found a couple of airhostesses in the 'Flèche Rouge' ('Red Arrow'). This was a highly amusing bar filled with some of the craziest people I have ever seen. We sat around a small table in our uniforms, dripping with sweat, and chatted to the girls. Mama Fanta arrived in a light-rose shawl to show us a few tricks. I could see her breasts through the light material hanging like a couple of wet socks over her scaly belly. She was over 70 years old and had clearly lost the plot. She hadn't any teeth. I know of a couple of blokes who returned saying that oral sex was an experience to forget. She sat on a chair and opened her legs to reveal her vagina. Someone gave her a 50-franc piece and it soon disappeared inside her. She produced a Durex from somewhere like magic and soon it was over her head and inflated. I watched with interest the reaction of the airhostesses, but I was disappointed to see that there was not a blink or shocked expression. Geordie used Mama's vagina as a cigarette holder, which we found amusing. It was to be another year before I managed to find a willing white French girl.

We toured for the summer and visited Auday again. It would be the last time for many years. War was slowly approaching and soon the country would change.

In September I started a six-week sniper course in the

desert. We slept on camp beds in ten-man tents. Each morning we would go for a run around the hills, which would nicely dehydrate us for the day. The sergeant major in charge was a heavily built and very scary Italian boxing champion. He had been in the Legion 25 years and it showed: consequently, he rationed us to one litre of water a day. The temperature was in the forties. Continuously thirsty, we fired round after round on the ranges, each time running back and forth to check the results. My mouth tasted bitter continuously – a sign of dehydration. After a couple of weeks the sergent-chef relented and allowed us two bottles a day.

I made a suit with Hessian, which I wore while we practised stalking around the wadis. It broke the shape of my shoulders well but it was too hot to wear for long periods. It was a slow process. Each movement was laboriously slow so as not to draw attention to ourselves, because movement catches the eye. We navigated around the surrounding hills every couple of days and perfected our pacing and map reading. There was a large hill to the rear of the camp that rose for about 400 metres, which we would have to run up for the slightest misdemeanour.

For the final exercise we spent three days navigating around the dessert. I was with a Moroccan and a Frenchman who were both good men. During the night we patrolled with our sniper rifles to specified rendezvous. During the day we hid in the rocks. We were the Grey team. On the radio the transmissions were brief, which was to avoid interception from the enemy.

'Grey.'

Each sniper team was given a colour for a call sign. A response from the base:

'Grey.'

'Received ... co-ordinates 234 543.'

'Grey ... new co-ordinates 234 632 ... read back.'

'234 632.'

We had been given our last RV. It was six kilometres away. We packed our kit. We didn't need much to survive. We had three water bottles and three days' rations. Our bodies were used to being dehydrated. We could work on little water. I carried a couple of magazines, each holding ten rounds, and my Musette (small rucksacks which we used for short-term operations) contained a piece of canvas to sleep on. I had a personal radio for transmission and the others had the team one for back to base. We carried nothing else. We didn't need it. My photocopied 1:100,000 map was difficult to read at night, but we managed to find our way to the RV. We were given the task of watching for a target in a grid square.

We stalked into an area where we could see the location the target would pop up sometime in the next 24 hours. We were in position so we waited ... and waited. I was tired but we had to be alert and ready for the shot. It would pop up for only 30 seconds. We would have to be quick. We discussed the distances and mentally logged them. I partitioned the ground in front of us into layers and remembered the distance. Wherever it popped up we would be ready. Later that afternoon, just as the sun was beginning to set, a target appeared about 400 metres away. I turned the dial to 400 and added a couple of clicks for the angle. I would aim high as I was shooting from a height.

'321 Feu!'

Our volley echoed through the open spaces. The target fell and we waited for the transmission.

'Gris.'

'Gris.'

'Return to base.'

We sneaked away and returned. Mission over. Six weeks in the desert and I was looking forward to a cold drink and a decent wash. We received our snipers badges and drank a cold beer before returning to camp.

Back in camp we hardly had time to unpack before configuring the wagons for the standby platoon. We were on standby for the next week. There was always a platoon ready to deploy if needed. While on standby, we would be given jobs to do around the camp and train. In the evening I went to the foyer to chat with a few of the lads. We had a little English mafia going. Dutch also joined in. He was a happy small lad with terrible acne scars on his face. We were sat there one evening when all of a sudden he blurted it out:

'I've got **AIDS**.'

He was visibly gutted and tears welled up in his eyes. We sat around in stunned silence. I had heard of a few guys that had caught it, but this was the first time it had happened to a friend of mine. I didn't know what to say, but soon it turned into a standard joke and we started to take the micky, asking him if we could have his boots and money, as he would not need them!

Dutch left for France a few weeks later. I was to be on sentry next to the airport the day he left. I told him I would flash a red torch at the plane when it took off. He wrote to me a month later informing me that he had seen the light. I never heard anything again. He was 22 years old.

We returned to CECAP to do the commando course that we had missed due to Operation Godoria. We slept in small open huts and it was nice to be by the sea. Each morning we ran around the desert, forward rolling and doing press-ups. I was experienced now and took enjoyment in beating the newer lads in the unarmed combat sessions. The instructor was a fit muscular man from the Dominican Republic. The course was similar to the one I had done in Mont Louis. The assault courses went around the hills to the north but the aquatic one was different. It began with a death slide into the sea followed by a swim under or climb over a series of floating obstacles. This was hard work but enjoyable in the crystal blue water.

We spent a couple of days jumping from helicopters that would slowly cruise along the coast. I sat on the edge of the door. Thirty feet below, the sea was dark and deep. The trick was to make sure you landed straight and with both feet together. Water may seem like a soft landing but from that height it could kill you. I waited for the tap on my shoulder, slid off the ramp and fell for a few seconds. Silence. I crossed my arms and waited for the impact. I had leant forward slightly and upon hitting the water the wind was knocked out of me. Back on the shore I examined the huge bruise on my torso. Next time I made sure I was straight. Sometimes a little pain teaches, like a child soon learns not to touch the fire.

For the final exercise, using live ammunition, we infiltrated to the ranges. We marched up the mountains to Arta and returned back towards the coast. This took a couple of days. The marches were always long and hard but I was used to them now. I still carried very little but this time I had the machine-gun. In the winter I would carry a sleeping bag. We arrived under the cover of darkness to the waiting Zodiacs. I was in the front with the machine-gun. We didn't have to paddle this time as we had forty-horsepower outboard engines. I mounted the gun on the bow and tied it down ready for the beach assault. We approached towards the bay. The black sand glistened like varnish under the moonlight. Among the tank hulls and debris I saw the silhouette of a couple of targets. I was now used to working under the cover of darkness. With experience you can see anything unnatural, smell anything human and know your friends simply from their shadowy outline and the way they walk.

The light pop of the flare from the snipers soon turned into a bright orange glow. I was in range and started firing short bursts of two or three, as they are more accurate. The boat bounced up and down with the waves. I could see my tracer rounds impact all around the hillside. I would have to try to time my bursts with the rocking of the boat. I saw the red spark of my tracer burning next to the target so I was happy with that.

We beached the Zodiacs on the sand and ran forward into cover behind some metal hulls. I moved into a position to give covering fire towards the targets in depth. The group on my left advanced to the next available cover and began to put the rounds down. On the high ground to the left I could see the muzzle flashes from the snipers. They were using the new light-intensifying night sight, which was very accurate. I had better results with it than with the daylight optical lens. I could hear the zip of the rounds as they whizzed over my head. I gathered up my banded 7.5 link, a belt of rounds for the AAA machine-gun and ran behind the sergeant. He put me down in a position and told me to engage the furthest targets. My heart was pumping. I was tired from the march but I didn't feel it now. The adrenaline was rushing through my veins. I clipped on a new belt and let rip a few more bursts. Mac popped up with the 89-millimetre rocket launcher, checked his back-blast area and let the missile off down the range. The whole area was briefly illuminated with the explosion.

We were on the move again. My knees were bleeding from the rocks and sand was getting in the wounds. We took the final position and prepared to destroy the material left behind. We had prepared the charges a couple of days earlier and we had cut the fuse wire to burn for five minutes. A few kilos of TNT were placed on a tank hull and the fuse was lit. We had five minutes to exfil. We ran back to the boats while the snipers kept watching for any more targets. As the boats took us out to sea we looked behind to witness the flash of the demolitions before hearing the deep rumble a second later.

We returned to the base and got on some wagons. I thought to myself that it was finished. Suddenly, the wagons stopped and there was a lot of shouting outside.

The canopy was opened and a familiar face of one of the Brits brandishing an AK47 ordered us to get out. We were captured. As I got out of the wagon I was jumped on by a group of men. I struggled and grinned as I heard the groan from one of my assailants as I hit him in the balls. There were too many. I was dragged into a small derelict building where I was happy to see the rest of the lads, who were lying on their chests with their hands tied behind their backs. Their legs were tied to their hands so they could not move. I was pushed to the ground and bound tightly. It was an uncomfortable position to be in. The bindings rubbed my wrists and I began to lose sensation in my hands. We lay there like that until the morning. From the wall above I heard a familiar voice again. It was one of the medics – an Englishman. He grinned and started to pour tea on my head. Each time he did it he said, 'Oooops! Sorry, Sloane.' I strained my neck to look up and grin.

One by one we were taken from the room. I was the last one. I was absolutely drained but I was used to this feeling. I was dragged outside and released. An instructor was there and immediately I was doing push-ups. My arms were stiff and my fingers had seized up. I struggled to do the push-ups but I could crawl through the dust as he asked.

'Get up!'

I jumped up and he presented a gloved hand. I started to punch. I punched and kicked the pad on his hand for a few minutes. Every now and then an adversary would pop up from behind a rock and I would have to defend myself.

'Forward roll!'

He barked the order and I immediately fell forward. We didn't roll using our hands, as we would probably be holding a weapon; so we curved our backs and stooped low to lessen the impact of rolling on our necks and spines. At the end of the roll I used the momentum to stand up and face my opponent. My legs were shoulder length apart. I was careful never to cross them, as this would weaken my fighting stance. I raised my clenched fists and with all my lungpower screamed and shouted:

'En garde!'

A left followed by a right and then a kick to the glove.

'Plaquage au sol!' 'On the ground!'

I forced my legs back and broke my fall with my hands, landing where my feet had been. Dust turned to mud between my fingers with sweat. I began to feel them again. I did some more press-ups.

'Get up!'

'Forward roll!'

'Romp! Romp! Crawl! Crawl!'

'Hands in your pockets!'

I wriggled in the dust over the rocks with my hands in my pockets. I could taste the dirt in my mouth. The wheezing I heard sounded almost alien … as if it wasn't my own breath. As if I was outside of myself. I needed air and wished it would stop.

'Get up!'

'Punch! … Kick! … Punch! … Kick! … Forward roll!'

This was one of the hardest sessions of my life and the heat wasn't helping. My eyes were blurred with sweat and fatigue. I couldn't focus on the corporal. I was beginning to swagger from left to right and lose my step. I was fucked. Completely fucked!

'Forward roll!'

I slumped and rolled, struggling to get back up. I was angry. I now hated this man. I got up and punched some more, imagining the glove was his face. I arrived at a rope and he gave me a knot to tie. Still swaying I tried to concentrate through my blurry eyes.

'C'est fini.'

I staggered off to the others and had a drink. I sat quiet for a few minutes staring into space to regain myself. We joked about it and laughed at each other's condition. I collected my second commando badge.

.... CHAPTER 9

We returned to Djibouti town and spent a couple of weeks doing duties. Back in camp I was called to see the lieutenant. I marched in and saluted. I quite liked him. He had trouble keeping up with us on the morning runs but he would push himself so hard, to the point that he would wretch. He was determined to gain our respect. We didn't mind that. I liked a man who would try his best: after all, what more can a man do? I had been a legionnaire for three years, so I was pleased when he told me that I had been selected to do the corporal promotion course in CECAP. I knew that soon I would be left alone. That soon my days of cleaning the toilets and standing at the gate would be over.

We paraded outside the CECAP car park early on the Monday morning with our sacs à dos Bergans on our backs. The temperature at that time in the morning, just before the sun rose, was quite cool for Djibouti – it was about 30 degrees in the early hours. We loaded up into the wagons and were dropped off eight kilometres up the wadi. Thirty of us stood on the start line. I looked around me. There were a few familiar faces from the company and the 2nd REP. We would have to work together and yet we were in competition, because the higher you were placed on the course the sooner you were promoted. The adjutant stood in front of us:

'This, as you know, is the *Peloton* [the promotion course]. If you want to be a corporal you must be stronger, fitter and more knowledgeable than your subordinates. You must learn what you are taught. This will not be easy. Your first test is the 8-kilometre TAP, which you will all pass eventually.'

On the start line we had a nervous piss before beginning. The sergeant had sent us up a hill and back to warm up. I pulled up my socks and folded them over the buckle of my boots, since it distracted me to hear the rhythmic chinking as I ran. The whistle blew and the stopwatch started: we raced off, but it wouldn't be long before the first would slow down with the heat. The sun was warming now and the sweat had already soaked my shirt. It felt quite cool and comfortable. I didn't pace myself but sprinted as fast as I could until I had to slow a little. It would be a while before I realized that if I kept the pace a little slower and steady, I would soon catch the ones that sprinted at the beginning. My sac à dos rubbed on my back, and the dust created sores that soon began to sting with the sweat. Thirty-nine minutes later five of us arrived. We walked around in circles trying to catch our breath while we waited for the rest to come in. A couple arrived in the sergeant's P4 (a four-wheel-drive vehicle). They had collapsed. In my pride I was disgusted with this. I had no time for people who couldn't keep up. We were legionnaires and we didn't give up. They were taken to the medical centre, refilled with intravenous liquids and then they continued with the day's work.

We showered and sat down for the first lesson. The lessons would go on for days. I wrote what was being said as it sounded. I was amazed when the Frenchman next to me kept asking me what the instructor had said.

We learnt all the characteristics of all the weapons. I could recite weights, lengths, maximum and minimum ranges. I knew all the frequencies, all the antennas, all the part names and numbers. We learnt every minute detail; we learnt battle first aid and practised putting drips into each other. When we weren't in the classroom we were patrolling or learning how to position mines and traps.

Before each meal we had the apéritif ... the rope ... pull-ups ... sit-ups ... and press-ups. It was too hot to work in the midday sun. In the afternoon, when the sun was still high, the instructors would have a little siesta while we carried rocks up and down a 200-metre hill to the rear. If at any time someone messed up we would all have to run up and down it – which I found annoying – but we soon learnt that we had to work as a team to get things done. I resented the people who messed up, but soon I helped them for my own ends. I didn't want to run up and down the hill, so I made sure they didn't mess up. In the evenings we marched each other around singing songs or wrote our reports, which would take us to the early morning.

It was my turn to be group commander. Flaubert, my second-in-command, patrolled to the rear to ensure we didn't lose anyone on the way. I turned around:

'Dix mètres d'espace.' 'Spacing ten metres.'

One by one the message was passed down the line. I checked my bearings, followed the arrow and headed for the lion-shaped rock that I could see far in the distance. I was happy with that, put my compass away in my shirt pocket and closed the button. 'Always check your kit, always close your pockets and pouches.' Stein's words always came to mind when I had to concentrate. When I first joined the REP I had lost a blank firing attachment – a screw-on metal bracket that attached to the barrel of the Famas. This bracket blocked the barrel, which enabled enough backpressure to hit the bolt and re-cock the weapon. Without this we would be forced to re-cock before each shot when firing blanks. I had been sentenced to a week in prison for my crimes.

We stopped for a drink and a little food. I didn't carry a stove, as there was no need: the tins of beans and bacon were always warm in the heat. The cavalry sergeant approached. I looked at his long, curly moustache, which he twirled while he spoke:

'Sloane: the ambush position in Grid 786 231.'

I checked my map and he pointed with his pencil to the dry riverbed. It was two kilometres to the north. I checked my watch and it was nearly half-past four. We would have to move a little to be there before dark. I wanted to see the area in daylight before positioning the mines. I signalled to the lads to pack up, ensuring that the jerrycan of fuel was changed around and that the heavy loads were distributed.

'Check your pockets and pouches ... got all your kit?'

Stein's words had become my own. We moved off and Flaubert checked the ground to ensure that we had not left anything behind.

The ambush site was on a vehicle track in a wadi. I knew the area, as this was a live range that we frequently used. We were using live explosives on this one, but first, I needed to plan my assault. This was an ambush, it was up to us to decide how to implement it according to the layout or the terrain: it was to test my ability to destroy the enemy. I took Flaubert with me for a look, while the rest of the group rested for a while. He had been in the French army and the 2nd REP. He didn't need to try on this course – he knew all the stuff already. We looked at the track and decided the best way to stop the vehicle was with one of the round ten-kilogram anti-tank mines. There, of course, was not going to be a vehicle but we were going to play for real and pretend that there was.

The track was a couple of metres from a vertical rock face. This would be an ideal place to cache the jerrycan, which we had prepared back in camp. I had filled it two-thirds full with petrol and a third with motor oil, so it became a giant Molokov cocktail. On one side we attached an improvised MIAPED (*Mine Antipersonnel d'Effet Dirigé*, Anti-personnel Mine with Burst Effect, very similar to the British Claymore Mine) with tape. The MIAPED was a dinner-plate shaped anti-personnel mine. We had packed the back of the plate with plastic explosive and the front with a yellow resin in which we inset nuts, bolts and glass. We painted it with sandy coloured paint and rubbed dust into it while it was wet. This we placed against the rock face and camouflaged with a few rocks. I stuck an extra couple of blocks of TNT behind to help it off. This took care of one escape route.

On the other side we placed small circular individual anti-personnel mines. Small and easy to carry, they were concealed a centimetre below the surface. Stand on one and you could say goodbye to your leg and your nuts. We left the metal rings so that we could recover them later. For the sake of the exercise, we attached them together with detonating cord so that we could blow the lot in one go. The det cord would explode at seven kilometres a second, which made it virtually instantaneous. Right: the track and sides were covered.

I set up an issued **MIAPED** to the rear to finish off any runners. The issued ones contained 900 grams of explosive and 1,000 ball bearings that would fly at an angle of 60 degrees wide for about 100 metres. We set this one on det cord also. In a war situation we would set up the very light electrical wire zigzagging in the killing area. Break this light 'fishing line' and the mine would explode.

As we placed the mines we drew a map, logged bearings, distances and the locations of the explosives. This I would have to write up in my report. It was necessary if we needed to recover the mines once they had been laid.

I attached all the det cords together with tape and timed a piece of *mèche lente* (slow-burning fuse) to burn for 60 seconds. On the end of this I crimped a detonator and taped it to the det cord. We were ready to go. I checked the wooden targets and counted them. I needed to record the enemy kills. With my Opinel penknife I sliced though the fuse and inserted three matches from the ration boxes. A quick nod from the sergeant: the matches spluttered before coming to life, and the puff of smoke from the cord meant it was burning. We sneaked off around the corner to meet the rest. Seconds after the quick head count the ground shook, the noise deafened us and a beautiful bright flash illuminated the surrounding rocks.

Scattered holes of all shapes burnt through the wood of the previously undamaged targets: the effect on a human being would be devastating. The burning oil clung to the rocks and made the fire last longer. Small craters were left from the small anti-personnel mines, while the targets to the rear were splattered with ball bearings. If you drove into that ambush you would be lucky to get out alive.

We packed up to return to base. Every time I stopped to check my map I hid under my poncho to hide the light. 'Light. Noise. Movement. Go slow at night.' Stein's words were back – I was glad to have worked with the man. We arrived back at first light, ready to meet the other groups for the assault course before going back to the class-room.

That evening I wrote my reports after a couple of hours marching the lads around and singing songs. Three copies of each sheet had to be written. Flaubert helped me with the grammar, although they didn't mind if it wasn't all correct, so long as there was no crossing out. The company address was fitted exactly into a five-centimetre square; the margins had to be exactly one and a half centimetres from the edge of the page and the lines of writing on the blank paper had to be straight. This was a long, painstaking task that none of us enjoyed, particularly those who were not native French speakers.

I became incredibly fit during this course. In the mornings we either ran, did the TAP or the assault course, and each time a couple of men would collapse with heat exhaustion. There weren't any medical withdrawals on the course unless you had really done some damage. During daylight hours we learnt about explosives and the machine-guns, testing each other on our skills.

The sergeant major running the course was a gentle man, who had mellowed with age. He had been in the Legion for over 30 years: his wrinkled walnut skin and wiry body would leave 25-year-olds behind in the morning runs. He had done his promotions course in Djibouti in 1962, and he was running it exactly the same. Some things don't change. But in a way it made us proud that we were being treated the same as our predecessors, that we were having it just as hard and that the standards didn't drop.

A couple of weeks into the course we ran the 22 kilometres uphill from Arta Beach to Oueah, where we did the rope test just as the course had done in 1962. I hauled myself up with my legs straight out in front of me, up and down three times. We had to climb the six-metre rope in under six seconds to pass. I would never be that fit again; the heat and continuous beastings defined every muscle in my body. I had changed from the ten-stone skinny kid that walked through those gates into a hard-skinned man.

We revised every night and timed ourselves stripping the weapons while blindfolded. The pistol was easy but the .50 Browning machine-gun was a nightmare. But we had rehearsed and learnt to feel every individual piece, finishing off by feeling for the breech to do the fire-no-fire checks. The thinner gauge placed between the bolt and the barrel would allow the firing mechanism to work, while the thicker one would not. We finished the course with written tests and the usual physical ones. I knew all there was to know about all the weapons and kit I would use. Soon I would be passing my knowledge to others.

The three-day march back to Djibouti City is nothing more than a blur. We slept and drank little, plodding night and day through the wadis. A few men had to be put in the wagon and were not to be seen again. They had failed on the last hurdle. We arrived back on a Wednesday evening in time for the weekend and going crazy in the town.

.... CHAPTER 10

I had been away from the company two months, so I was happy to be back, knowing that I would soon be a corporal and that I would no longer have to do the menial jobs. I met Mac in the foyer before going for a few beers on the beach, where we met up with the English speakers and arranged a meal in the Vietnamese restaurant.

We were shown to a room at the rear of the restaurant; the staff had learnt from previous visits to separate us from other customers, as things often became rowdy. All eyes followed us as we made our way through the tables to disappear behind a curtain. I consulted the menu and ordered 12 bottles of Bordeaux rouge and an array of *nems* (a delicious rolled pancake that came with a vinegar sauce), sweet and sour and some other dishes. The food was good for Djibouti and it was always worth a visit when we had the chance.

It was the first trip in town for a couple of guys who had just finished their training in Castelnaudary. Jim was an east Londoner and had been with us for a few weeks. He looked (and was) hard as nails; the array of tattoos on his face and neck adding to the effect. He had been a skinhead in London, and from his appearance it was apparent that he was handy with his large fists. They were always clenched ready for a fight, but to us he was a friendly mate once you got to know him. His square jaw and scarred, mean features would scare people, which generally deterred them from light conversation. Earlier on in the day, the song 'Another One Bites The Dust' by Queen was playing. He grinned as he told the story of how he and his friends would drive around in a BMW in London with the song blasting out, looking for 'niggers'.

'We would drive about and every time we fucking saw one of the fucking black cunts we would pop our shotgun out of the window and point it at them, singing ...' – the corners of his mouth curled towards his chin when he grinned and his thin lips almost disappeared – '... another one bites the dust!'

I laughed and sipped a little wine. I could tell that tonight was going to end in trouble. Still, the balls of battered chicken were nice, so I enjoyed a couple more, waiting to see what would happen next. We were now very drunk and emotion would soon begin to run high.

An Irish lad stood up, knocking his chair onto the floor, and made a toast to the 'Legion Paras', spilling wine over the tablecloth as he did so.

'Au REP.'

We clinked our glasses and gulped down a little more red. It was a foolish thing to do and I will never understand his reasoning, but Martin stood up, toasted his glass and slurred:

'Paras are shit!'

Mac and I looked at each other. We didn't need to speak. Our eyes showed it all; the disbelief that he had made such a comment among the present company. Paddy was holding a half-full wine bottle. A flash of red glass followed by a splash of red on the white tablecloth, and Martin's face exploded while his nose decided to point to the left as if indicating to his ear that something was wrong. Plates and glasses toppled and the table shook. Blood dribbled into the rice while Martin slumped in the plate with his eyes closed.

'Fucking hell! Martin, you're making a mess on the table.'

We laughed, picked him up and put him in a chair in the corner. Mac checked his breathing before grabbing his nose between his thumbs and putting it back in place. We carried on with the party and downed a few more beers. Startled faces followed us out of the restaurant as we left in a long line through the narrow spaces between the tables. Mac had the unconscious body of Martin over his shoulder, blood dripping from his face down the back of his socks.

Martin said a few things to upset some people. He began to find himself alienated, but nobody cared. You either join the Legion and get used to it, or you fuck off. We didn't care. Join us or leave. Soon after he went to the Padre to spill his heart out, and he returned to France never to be seen again.

'Le Perroquet', 'The Parrot', was one of the small bars on the side streets. Paddy jumped on a table and pulled his trousers down, revealing a couple of eyes tattooed on his buttocks. He was given a full bottle of beer and he popped a length of toilet roll up his anus. I looked up at him and started the countdown:

'3 ... 2 ... 1.'

I lit the paper with a lighter and he began to drink. The flames crept towards his butt and he thrust his pelvis forward to gain time. A metre of toilet paper burns in seconds. You are only allowed to remove the burning paper once you have drunk the beer. He dropped the bottle and frantically patted out the flames. We laughed hysterically. The bar had an upstairs balcony, which soon had 12, naked, drunken legionnaires swinging, with burning paper hanging from their arses.

I can't remember leaving the bar and picking up the niah. I woke the next morning with my tongue stuck to the inside of my mouth. The sheet clung to my body with sweat. I knew it was late because of the heat. I looked around the room wondering where I was. The room was homemade with bits of corrugated iron and scraps of wood. The young girl in bed next to me groaned and put her hand on my thigh. I had woken in *Bala Bala* (shanty town), where white eyes were not allowed. It was forbidden by the locals and by the Legion. Men had gone in there and never been seen again.

La Croix, a former French Para, was still in the medical centre recovering from his injuries. The driver of the taxi that he had taken in the early hours of the morning hadn't said much, preferring to chew his qat and get on with his fare. Qat was a leaf that the locals chewed, adding to it throughout the day until they had a mashed ball of green bulging through their cheeks. This was a drug of some kind. After midday there was not a sane soul to be found; most of the men in town flying high.

La Croix slouched in the back and closed his eyes. He woke when the taxi stopped, finding himself alone in the back. The first thud caused the roof to crumple and the second smashed the window to his right. Shocked into soberness, he jumped through the gap to the driver's seat. An iron bar smashed the windscreen hitting him in the face while the crowd cheered. Fumbling for the keys he ducked down, reversing out towards the main road. The crowd gave chase while the wheels spun in the dust, and the smell of the burning clutch filled the cab. He left Bala Bala behind him and sped back to camp. He'd had a narrow escape.

In the corner of the room sleeping in a chair and on the floor were a couple more girls. I politely refused a breakfast of cold wot. After the enormous amount of alcohol the previous evening I could not stomach dirty fingers and rotten camel for breakfast. They told me the Legion military police were looking for me. I had a couple of hundred metres to go to the main road. Alone, I walked with eyes burning holes in my back. Although hung-over, I was suddenly fully alert, walking straight ahead with my eyes darting everywhere. I checked the dark areas and tried to keep an eye for shadows behind me. Fortunately, it was daylight and unlikely that I was going to have any trouble. Back at camp I presented in front of the duty sergeant on the gate, fearing the worst. I was hoping for a cell and not a beasting. My singed uniform was covered in blood, beer and dust. I had lost a few of the badges and my shoes were brown with dirt. He leant back on his chair and contemplated. I waited. Hurry up for fucks sake! The silence added to my fear. I knew I was in trouble: it felt like I was at school again, in front of the headmaster for bunking off. That feeling when all the blood runs to your toes and your stomach feels like it's a washing machine.

'En slip!' 'Down to your pants!'

I stripped off. It was a good sign. He led me through the back to the taule. I was led into a small room, which was about two metres by three. On the far wall high up was a small barred window, letting just enough light in to see the metal bucket in the corner. Besides the bucket, the empty concrete floor finished the décor nicely. He handed me a bottle of tap water and slammed the door behind him, leaving a lingering echo followed by silence in the dark.

I sat on the floor and looked around, wondering how long I would be in here. I knew O'Neil, an Irish lad, was still in here somewhere. He had been in solitary for a month but he would not leave for another 30 days, with a nice beard to show us all.

'The Mac Bar' stretched 50 metres and was usually packed with locals and soldiers alike. O'Neil ordered a drink. When the barman returned, O'Neil grabbed him by the throat and shoved the barrel of a stolen Russian Marakov pistol from the Godoria Operation into his mouth. The bar didn't go silent, although the barman didn't say a word, he just stood there looking at O'Neil with his eyes wide open like two footballs floating in a dark pool.

Click.

Click.

Click.

Nothing! The old pistol had misfired, which was fortunate for the rest of the bar. If O'Neil had started, who knows when he would have finished? A couple of lads wrestled him to the ground and the military police arrived. O'Neil had been in here since.

I sat and stared at the little window. It was past midday now, and the room was like an oven. My bad head and dehydration from the night before made it feel worse. I sipped some of the unfiltered tap water, which tasted and smelt like rotten eggs. I looked through the clear plastic at tiny white mites swimming around. They moved in fast, short, random bursts around each other as if they were dancing. The water was only drinkable when it was very cold or frozen as the taste was so bad that a long gulp would make my stomach wretch. You were guaranteed diarrhoea when you drank it, but beggars cannot be choosers. I sipped a little and almost threw up. Resigned to my situation, I lay on the floor for the day in the heat, kind of half asleep. The outline of sweat around my body from the warm floor reminded me of the chalk outline of corpses on American cop films.

I dreamt of O'Neil not having a misfire and shooting the barman's brains out. I didn't care. Life was cheap in Africa. I didn't care about anything. We were in it together: I had changed and lost what compassion I may have had. Three years earlier I had been a young innocent boy of 18. I was now a killer. I didn't care for the goats we killed. I didn't care for the dying people we saw in Godoria. I didn't think any more; I didn't need to. I just wanted to drink and have sex and kill. I had been transformed and I liked it. The aggression in me had been built up to the point that it boiled in my blood. I could feel it through my body ... and my body said, 'Fuck you.' It said, 'Go on! Fucking try it!'

My young mind had been transformed. If I'd had any inherent good in me before it was now locked away in a little box deep down and I would not find it for a good few years.

A sponge soaking up water.

We are all products of our surroundings. How we are treated reveals itself in the way we treat others. It would take a lot of self-reflection in years to come for me to realize that. Until then, my life would reveal itself in my aggression. I was now a tool. An ideal non-thinking killing machine: 'Fuck you!'

I drifted in and out of sleep, shifting position every now and then to get my blood running in a different direction. The day was long, my mouth was dry and my head banged with dreams of guns and brains. I closed my eyes, concentrating on the warm air as it entered my nostrils, and I found myself aware of the warmth and blood in my hands. I was alive. I could feel it. I wasn't hungry. I wasn't really thirsty. I felt nothing and the nothingness felt good. Like after a fight and the adrenaline dies down but your body still remembers the pain, or when you narrowly escape in a car accident. It was that flying around the room feeling while your body lay numb with drink. It was that feeling of floating when your body is too tired to move but too awake to sleep. It was those feelings that meant something. It was the knowledge that I was still here.

I was glad when the sun set, and I was left in the dark to think. My mind began to wander. I began to plan my leave in a year's time. I would go and visit my dying father in Spain and see my brothers. Dad was dying; we were all dying. We played the game of life but we could not win. I don't find it sad, life is cheap ... we all die. I had accepted death.

I dreamt of my father working on his swimming pool. I had mixed concrete for him for six months in Spain while he taught me how to reinforce it with iron bars. When I had the chance I spent my £5 wages on a few beers on the coast. When he had finished with me he bought me a ticket back to London and gave me £50. I found myself in London at 17 years old, with 50 quid, nowhere to live and no job. Cheers Dad! I was being approached by an old man asking me out to a restaurant, and if I wanted to stay around his place. I looked at him and knew exactly what his game was. My boyish features letting me down again. 'Fuck you.'

I woke and sat in the dark and thought some more. My head was a little better. I sipped some more toilet water. It was nearly empty. The concrete floor didn't bother me. I had been in the desert for months sleeping on rocks and stones – I could sleep anywhere. I slept some more but this time I shivered through the night.

Two days later I was released. I had begun to get used to my cell. I wasn't annoyed during my time alone on the concrete in my pants. I had accepted it. The only thing on my mind was whether I was going to get any more water. I had accepted it and would have been happy to stay. What else could they do to me? Put me in solitary!

I saw the captain and was given probation, as it was the first time I had really been in trouble with the 13 DBLE and I had just finished my course. I think he thought the 'hole' was good enough punishment. I was promoted a week later. I had finished high in the course so I received my stripes early.

I was a corporal and now it was my turn to dish it out ... or so I thought. This attitude lasted a few weeks. Some new lads arrived in the platoon so I set them cleaning the toilets and showers. Another corporal told them to stop so I left it, and I was annoyed at not being able to treat them the way I had been treated. A Chinese lad laughed in the ranks so I punched him in the jaw. A Bulgarian that spoke English told me that I was 'losing it' and he was right. This was the new me.

'Fuck you.' The words were not in my mind but in my whole being. I'd had enough and I was ready to kill for the sake of killing.

A few weeks later we went to the ranges near Arta for some battle drills. I was in charge of my half-group. I felt the hot sun through my shirt as I lay and looked at the targets that we were going to attack. The sergeant positioned the 1952 7.5-millimetre light machine-gun to the right for covering fire. I saw the Chinese lad carry it up the hill and thought, '1.165 metres long, 9.9 kilos, fed with 200 round belts, range with the tripod he is carrying 1,000 metres, and a cyclic rate of 700 rounds a minute.' I knew every detail from my CME (Cadre Militaire Elémentaire), my promotions course.

We approached as close to the enemy as possible and waited for the signal on the radio:

'Premièr groupe en avant.'

A short burst from high on the right and we moved forward. I looked towards the sergeant to see when he would go to cover. As he dived down I shouted to the others:

'Plaquage au sol!' 'Hit the deck!'

One more bound and we would be ready for the final charge. When we were so close we felt it was better to just get stuck in. No time to waste: get in there quick. I switched my Famas selector lever to change from a full burst of 5.56-millimetre rounds to short bursts of three, which were more effective and ammunition efficient, and pushed the safety catch to the left before charging. Rocks split and puffs of dust appeared where my strike hit the targets, before I kicked them over and stabbed them with my bayonet. The half-rotten corpse of a camel was a couple of metres behind, so I ran forward and screamed, thrusting the blade through the rotten flesh – each time I twisted and heard the ribs crack. Again and again I stabbed, my eyes glazing over; kill, thrust and twist, kill, thrust and twist, kill. Fuck you ... Fuck you! I realized the shooting and shouting had stopped when I could hear the damp thud of my bayonet in the flesh of the ribcage, which had broken and gone soft, and my team was looking at me:

'C'est comme ça en faire! Putain chameau rigole à moi!' 'That's how we do it, fucking camel laughing at me!'

This attracted a laugh from the lads and a few 'he's mad' type comments. I didn't give a fuck any more. Humanity and compassion were a thousand miles away, in a three-bed semi with an old man washing his car outside on a Sunday morning. Here in the desert, dripping with sweat in front of a rotten carcass, I am now somebody else. I am no longer part of it. I have been changed and I will forever look on through a lens as an outsider.

We laughed. As we walked back to clean our weapons, Balic slapped me on the shoulder:

'Ça va caporal?'

'Oui, ça va bien … Tu sors c'est soir?' 'Sure, fine. You going out tonight?'

Balic was a good Hungarian friend of mine. I now outranked him but I had earned his respect by explaining to him my reasoning for putting him on duty twice in a row. There simply were not enough men available. It was unfortunate but if I explained it, it was appreciated. I no longer treated the lads the way I was treated. I preferred to keep them as friends.

I was drinking heavily. Mac and I would go to town and buy bottles of gin. I'd had a few fights with some of the regular French soldiers. They would start on us because they hated us, but they always ended up worse off. If a legionnaire was jumped upon it would not be long before the culprits were found and beaten. I stopped sleeping with prostitutes as they disgusted me, and instead I turned my hatred into a party trick. It wasn't hatred for the people. I wasn't racist – I just hated anything that was not a part of the Legion. Not a part of my family, my small new world. I would approach a niah in a bar and pretend to be a nice Frenchman. I could pull this off easily. I would then ask for a dance. While dancing I would let them fall back in my arms and then just drop them. They would land in a heap on the floor and we would laugh! This progressed to leading them by the hand, and then as I approached I would launch them across the dance floor. This lasted for a while until I picked one that was a little too light. She rocketed in mid-air to the mirrors in the background. On impact she slumped in a heap. I knew this would cause a riot ... we would often have riots. I stopped the 'party trick' from then on. It was a horrible thing to do but I didn't care at the time. 'Fuck you!' ... 'fuck you!' I was beyond caring. The drink and the heat were taking their effect. I was slowly beginning to lose all perspective on what I now consider to be a cushy western reality. The anger was growing, and the hate with it.

War had broken out in the North. The Afar rebels wanted independence. We were deployed to set up an observation post screen to the North.

Operation Escoutier was to observe the rebels and the Djiboutian army, assess their numbers and routine. We arrived a few kilometres past the flat plains of the Grand Bara, a long flat desert plain of about 50 kilometres in length, and set up a base. The wagons managed to climb the hills and get through the lava rocks, which covered the entire area. Initially, we didn't have any tents so we constructed shelters from the sun with rocks and camouflage nets. This was an *ouvert* (open) base so we weren't expecting any trouble. We deployed sentries anyway to keep a look out to the north.

For the next 30 days we dug defensive positions in the hot sun and slept in the dirt on the floor. The 'shit pits' were down the hill. As we dug them we took it in turns to see how many sandbags we could run up the hill with on our shoulders to make the laborious task in the sweltering heat a little less mundane.

In the evenings we prepared the fresh rations and cooked over a fire. There were four of us Brits in the platoon and we always drank after food. When the beer ran out we heated up the issued red wine, added sugar and fruit and made a 'Hot Wine'. Mac had been promoted so we all had a rank and therefore didn't need to mount the guard. Stokes was formerly an officer in the Royal Marines. It was soldiers like these that passed on knowledge from other armies to the lads (like myself) who had walked through the gates as civilians. He had suggested to the officers that I was promoted. It was good to have him on my side.

'So, Stokes, why did you become a *foutre foutre*?' Mac directed the question. I looked at the handsome chiselled features of Stokes, eagerly awaiting a reply. A foutre foutre is a legionnaire who is offered the choice to stay in the 4eme Regiment Etrangère for another 18 months after basic training, to act as a corporal, do the course and be promoted before joining a regiment. It was a system that I believe was designed to accommodate the lads joining who had previous military experience, although a few others had taken this route. It was a fast-track system for promotion. Become a foutre foutre and you could be a sergeant within four years. I was offered this when I finished training, but I declined because I didn't want to take any shortcuts. How could I lead without experience?

'Well, I didn't want to sweep floors and I knew from my time in the Marines that I could lead, so I took that option.' It was a fair answer. We respected him. He had been in the Legion eight years and was a very good leader. We were all good friends.

'Yeah but how did you get on when you turned up at the REP and you didn't have any time behind you?'

He leant forward and winked at us. I was interested to find out how.

'I called a kangaroo court.' A kangaroo court was a drunken trial of someone who had messed up in some way. It was something the English did within English circles. It was considered that if you were from the United Kingdom, a certain amount of excellence was required. Let the side down and you would be punished.

'I hung a man ... well I tried to from a door in the second company. But the nails came out. I found that if people thought you were mad they would respect you a bit.'

I could never be sure whether Stokes was still pretending to be nuts by the end of our two years, or whether he had actually become a bit crazy like the rest of us. At times when we were not allowed to go into town, he would escape over the barbed wire fence with us when he could quite easily have walked out the gate. Sometimes we found him muttering to himself about 'getting one before he left' (getting a local), as he walked the streets alone late at night.

The train from Paris to Marseille ran overnight when we returned to France a year later. Stokes was drunk and wanted a button from a French civilian's jacket, who adamantly refused to let him have it. Stokes pulled out a knife from his pocket and stabbed the man in the leg before cutting off the button and telling him:

'If you ever say a word I will find you and kill you.'

We still went out to the positions to observe and log during the day, while during the night we observed from closer to the base where there was more cover. Occasionally, we would patrol out for a few days and stalk up to observe the camps from the hills. It was while on one of these trips that Lamaz had found Lemois asleep on sentry. This was a serious offence. Back at the base camp Lamaz, a wiry man from Beirut, began to hand out his punishment.

He told me of the underground bars and the nightlife during the wars in the Lebanon. He said I should visit with him and, thinking back, I wish I had. He had hard pale scars on his arms and legs from when he was a child and had had to crawl around in hot shrapnel during the battles. He didn't care for anything. None of us did. Lemois forward rolled in the desert and crawled in the hot sun; Lamaz kept him going until he collapsed and we had to put a drip in him to sort him out. Don't fall asleep when mounting the guard!

It was difficult to lead people who had so much more experience in life. There were lads in the platoon who were in their thirties. I chose to explain to them why things were done and any punishment I gave, I did with them. This was usually press-ups. To my timing we would push them out. In this way I earned respect. A corporal had to be better and fitter. That is why you were chosen. I would ensure that I could run faster and knew my stuff. In the evenings before going out I would train, running and beasting myself. It was a matter of pride. But I didn't get my hands dirty any more. Do a menial task and a sergeant would grip you and tell you that you were a corporal not a legionnaire. It was a fine balance to keep everyone happy.

We were replaced a month later. For the next few months we spent 15 days on the operations and 15 training. After each tour we dismantled everything we owned and cleaned it. Every magazine was stripped, our *équipement* (webbing) dismantled, our Musettes and sacs à dos, all of the weapons – everything. I found this annoying to begin with, but it was just a way of making sure everything was clean, working and ready for the next trip. We would never know when a vital piece of equipment would fail because it wasn't looked after.

Each night that we were not on guard we were in the town or in the foyer drinking beer and watching the only local television channel, which broadcast the news in four languages each night. We laughed at the talent show on which a couple of hopeless hopefuls would stand on a school stage and try to sing, using balloons tied to their guitars for special effects.

Each morning we ran or did the assault course, followed by a sandwich and a beer in the foyer before work started at eight. Mac and I were still heavy drinkers: gin and tonic being our preferred beverage. We had met a couple of French girls in one of the nicer bars.

Isabelle wasn't a pretty girl but she was young and sexy and that was all I needed at that time. We spoke for a couple of hours one afternoon before I plucked up the courage to ask her straight if she fancied getting a local hotel to 'faire l'amour'. After all, I argued, we were both adults and both had needs. It started from there and continued until I left. I would see her every now and then. I knew she slept with other men but I didn't care: it wasn't love it was just sex.

Mac went home on leave. He had managed to get a second passport and with a few bribes in town he had an entry visa, which allowed him to leave the country. As he left I was green with envy. A few days later the French Navy took us to Tadjoura in the north. We set up a new camp and set about the ops. By the time we arrived in Tadjoura my forearm had swollen to the point that the only thing missing was Popeye's anchor tattoo. A doctor had a look and decided to slice it open to find out what was wrong: fortunately the medic arrive, injected me with antihistamine and the swelling from the unknown bite the previous evening subsided in hours. I didn't fancy getting patched up by that doc in a battle!

Mac returned a week later, exclaiming how everyone in England was so white. In his Musette he brought out two jars of Branston Pickle. This was a luxury far away from home. Together with the Eastern Bloc lads, we ate the lot on dry ration bread, but it could have been a fresh white loaf with large chunks of cheddar as far as I was concerned; it was Branston Pickle! It was home and memories that I had long forgotten, and it had never tasted so good. I had been in the desert for 14 months.

But the taste and memories soon faded. So I returned to the op, scanned the desert and waited for the rebels that never came. I was doing guard with the lads as we were told that they were on their way. Normally I would not, as it was seen to be wrong for a corporal to stag on. At times we would go on the ground and three NCOs would sleep while four legionnaires would spend most of the night awake. It was the done system. If someone was senior in any way, rank first, then time served or time promoted, then the work would be bypassed to the junior member. This was why so many people left after a few months: they worked like slaves, but the longer you stayed the easier it became; it was just a matter of sticking it out. We returned to Djibouti to drown our sorrows, disappointed that we hadn't been in action.

One evening the town was troubled and out of bounds from eight pm. As corporals, we spoke to the duty sergeant who said that if we stayed out he would mark us present so long as we were back in the morning. Mac and I were keen to get out as we had just returned from another two weeks in the field. We stayed in town while the others returned to camp for eight o'clock. The next morning we were called to the duty sergeant (a Frenchman) who had marked us absent after his false promises. Incensed, we gave him some verbal abuse before going to prison. When the working week started, we marched in to see the colonel and received 30 days each. On the Friday, another young English legionnaire joined us in the taule. He was the first to see the colonel. On exiting, he closed in and told us what happened:

'Well, I went in and did all the usual saluting and all that crap, then he started asking me if I took drugs! What does "tu foutre ma gueule ou quoi, mon colonel" mean, Sloane?'

Mac and I laughed, shaking our heads in disbelief.

'It means "Are you coming in my mouth or what, colonel!"'

'Oh! No wonder he went mad ... gave me 30 days!'

'Oh, we're fucked now also,' I said to Mac.

The 'guard tauler' had just changed and the new one wanted to make his mark. For the first week we ran around the assault course and got punished with press-ups around the camp, but this felt like a holiday compared to some of the previous things I had done. He soon calmed down and we settled into scheming a few things. We managed to get onto a painting detail to the rear of the camp near the outside barbed wire fence. The guard could not monitor us all, so considering we were corporals he let us do our own thing. Our own thing was to call some local lads to the fence, slip them some Djiboutian francs to get some drinks, and sup giant cans of cold Fosters behind a wall. During the day we would discretely meet with some of the Brits who would strate-gically place cases of beer in hiding places around the camp: prison wasn't too bad!

In the evenings, once we had cleaned the foyer (which doubled as a bar), we were locked up around half-past nine in a dark room with the other prisoners. We were stripped to our underpants and searched for beer, food or drink. We were, however, allowed to take in a jug of water. I replaced the water with gin and managed to supp away with Mac for a couple of hours. I had really begun to learn how to work the system.

Since the Berlin Wall had collapsed and communism no longer had its muffling blanket over the Eastern Bloc, hundreds of Hungarians, Poles, Romanians and Czechs had swamped the Legion gates.

In Paris the Fort de Nogent (the recruiting cell) was limited to two Polish people per day out of the 20 or 30 hopefuls that knocked on the heavy wooden gates each morning. We had a few in the platoon. These were hard men who had lived through hard times. I used to receive letters from Kovac's family as he was not allowed to write home. This was another way in which we could beat the system. Those that had a criminal background asked those of us that didn't to receive mail. Inside the envelopes addressed to me were family letters from loved ones in the East. Quite often the novelty of being in the West was evident. We would joke about the Poles and Hungarians taking photographs next to the Coke machine – a famous symbol of American capitalism and the Western world.

The heavily built Romanian corporal was an exceptional man. He appeared largely overweight, boasting a nice round potbelly, and yet he was one of the fastest and fittest men I had ever met. Behind his pocked features was a Neanderthal mind and a punch to match. On the previous 15-day desert trip he punched a Frenchman, who would have died if it were not for Mac pulling his tongue from his throat with forceps to open his airway. We were refilling the wagons when Balzac approached us, grinning from ear to ear; still drunk from the night before: these men from the Eastern Bloc could drink! They made their own vodka from any organic material they could find, and they would drink it straight from the bottle like beer, supping at least a bottle or two each before hitting the town.

'Mac ... Sloane.'

He pronounced my name 'Slooooownnee'. He moved between us and draped his heavy arms over our shoulders. He was sweating and reeked of vodka, grinning like a child about to tell a joke.

'Good night last night ... Me get niah!'

He thrust his pelvis to demonstrate while turning his head to get us both into the conversation.

'Moi ... say blow job.'

'She ... non! ... moi – bang!'

He demonstrated with his large fist a heavy punch into his palm and grinned some more, nodding his head in his own agreement.

'After ... she ... blow job.'

More nods and grins. Mac and I looked at each other, knowingly waiting for the next bit of the story.

'Moi ... want anal sex.'

'She ... non! ... moi – bang!'

Another graphic punch to the palm; cracking in the dry air.

'Moi ... anal. After she run down street naked ... blood

running from her arse!'

He straightened up and roared with laughter, slapping us both hard on the shoulders. I steadied myself a little and thought about the punch he had given Pele, the Frenchman, a few weeks earlier. Pele had upset him and was subsequently knocked out so cold by a single punch that he had swallowed his tongue. Mac and I looked at each other and shook our heads, grinning in disbelief. I didn't care for the girl: he was a legionnaire and we were in the Legion in Africa. Morals were something we lost on the way over. We thought that life and law were not taken seriously in these places and had assumed the same attitude.

The previous week he was bragging to us about his £2,000 fake Rolex watch, but we managed to convince him not to go back and buy a gold one for £6,000, telling him they would always break. We hadn't the heart to tell him the truth, and if we had I am sure he would have killed the shopkeeper.

These men were from a different culture. They were hard drinkers and fighters, always in the town partying. Some of them sent wages home and ran discothèques and brothels. Back in Poland the average wage was £12 a month. Here a corporal earned over a hundred times that. They would spend their five years and return millionaires.

A few of the English speakers got together for another night out. We started in the afternoon by the pool and soon made our way to the town for some food. I had a camel steak with rice. It was a red meat and very tough.

The horse steaks in the cookhouse were more succulent. My body had got used to continuously having *la chiasse* (diarrhoea). I hadn't had a solid toilet since France, and in the summer the lack of water left the toilets blocked; overflowing with flies and shit. We went to the 'Micky Bar' and ordered a bottle of gin. We ignored the niahs lurking in the corners. We left that for the guys who were still fresh and foolish. The owner was a small Frenchman who we would often see pottering around the place. We were drunk and about to leave the bar when he stopped us. We hadn't paid. In France you get a tab and pay at the end. We paid, but Jim was still having a heated discussion with the owner. I was waiting at the door and when I turned around I found Jim on the floor. Thinking the Frenchman had punched him and totally astounded that Jim had fallen, I dashed across in a flash, grabbed the patron in a headlock and smashed his nose to a bloody mush, while Jim got up and staggered. He had only fallen over drunk.

The niahs began to throw glasses and ashtrays. The damage was done so it was time to make a quick exit. Out on the street we walked away, but soon the girls were outside, babbling in their native tongue. Within seconds the commotion began and we had a lynch mob chasing us around the town. Bricks and bottles were thrown. It reminded me of a *Benny Hill* episode – there was always a chase at the end and every man and his dog joined in. In our case every tramp off the street, taxi driver and passer-by joined in to form an angry mob. We stopped to face them and they stopped. As soon as we turned our backs they began to run again. I was half expecting a noose to appear in front of the crowd. We laughed as we ran. They wouldn't come anywhere near us, but they would just chase! We were blocked off by a police van. We jumped in, slipped the coppers a few francs and like a taxi they drove us to the next bar. Money talks in Africa.

When we did have trouble with the local police we had a hilarious way of getting out of it. A guy had taken a photo of Paddy and then tried to make him pay for it. Paddy refused. He had not wanted or asked for a photograph. After a heated discussion, Paddy grabbed the camera, punched it and threw it away. It smashed on the floor. The police were called but they were not allowed to enter the bars. We made sure we had finished our drinks and agreed on the next bar to meet at: 'One ... two ... three ... go!'

We would rush onto the street, running in different directions. The police with their batons would try to catch us, but they weren't fast enough. Mac and I would laugh and stop to face them, but they wouldn't come near, as they were too afraid to approach the legionnaires. We would then carry on running and let ourselves into the next watering hole. We toasted the police from behind the door and carried on with the night's activities! Eventually, we would pay a few francs and be left alone, but the activity made a good evening a little better.

Once a year competitions were held and awards given for the best shots, tactical manoeuvres and fitness. We did the cross-country one morning and the assault course the next before travelling west to the wadis to go through the ranges. Tactical movement with vehicles can be slow and laborious in mountainous terrain. The platoon had four VLRA. We fully loaded them with ammunition, water and supplies. We could wash from the water tank under the chassis but we drank from jerrycans. We had one vehicle for the headquarters element, usually a lieutenant, sergent-chef and a signaller. In the other three we had six men in the rear and two up front. On the rear we mounted the .50 Browning. I would go on the ground with two or three weapons: my Famas assault rifle, my FRF2 sniper rifle and the Browning on the wagon.

The wadis wound like a snake through steep rocky hills. To enable us to advance safely we dismounted a section before each blind corner, and the section would patrol up to the high ground with all the weapons to check the area that was hidden to us in front. Once the all clear was given the other wagons could advance as far as the next vulnerable point. We would spend all day travelling a few kilometres. It was a combination of marching and driving. The terrain would change from mountains to rolling rock-covered hills to flat open desert. Each time we would use a different tactic to advance.

I slung my sniper rifle over my shoulder, and picked up my Mussette containing water and ammunition. I had a swig of warm liquid from my metal bottle before the steep climb. The rocks were hard and sharp, ripping through our light trousers and making us bleed. I was used to this by now. I continually had cuts and bruises on my legs from crawling and sleeping in the mountains. The sun was high and my back was soaking with sweat.

Just before the *crête* (the highest point on the hill), I crept forward with my assault rifle nestled on my shoulder. I wore my Hessian coat to break up my shape, but I used my assault rifle for the initial look, ready to react to close targets. I saw the ground to the front drop steeply.

From my first scan between two large boulders I saw nothing, but on my final check in the distance I saw a small head-and-shoulders target. I crawled back and briefed the sergeant who called up the other snipers. The enemy was 400 metres away. It was out of range for the assault rifle but fine for the snipers and the machine-gun. I crawled back to my position, and when the others had joined we started the range, the live firing exercise, with a single volley. I saw my strike was short and to the left. I aimed at the mirror image of my strike and fired again. This time I was on. If my initial calculations were wrong I preferred to aim off rather than wasting time trying to adjust the sights.

The judges to the rear were senior officers and sergeant majors from all parts of the Legion and the French Army, so we felt under pressure. We kept a steady rate of fire while the other three wagons advanced. The headquarters wagon was always in the middle to protect it. We advanced for another couple of hours before heading back to camp for a few well-earned cold beers. The days were long but I enjoyed them.

.... CHAPTER II

Summer 1992. It was cool in the classroom next to the *infirmerie* (infirmary). I sat behind a desk with 12 others, suturing a piece of pig's skin. For the past few weeks I had been studying medicine in every spare minute of the day, and I was beginning to wish that I hadn't spent so much time bunking off school and smoking cigarettes in the woods. The three months of theory would be followed by a four-week attachment to the local civilian hospital in Djibouti. This felt like it was going to be an interesting time. This would be the first time that I would interact with civilians. It was something new to me.

We practised on each other, and gained as much experience as possible by visiting the infirmary to curiously examine the horrible maladies that would arrive. Dave, an English corporal covered in tattoos, welcomed a scrawny Frenchman into the room and told him to lie down. He looked slightly nervous, as a group of us watched while he pulled out his penis to show Dave the cyst on his nuts. Dave called him a *clochard* (tramp) and injected the area around it with Lignocaine before carefully slicing down. He was keen to get the cyst as a whole so it would heal quicker. It was caused by an ingrown hair and was the size of a peanut. Dave showed us one that he had taken from a previous patient. It had yellow skin and looked a little like a miniature brain the size of a walnut! The Frenchman moaned so Dave punched him and told him to stop being a fanny.

'Putain … clochard!' 'Whore … Tramp!'

Dave pointed out the crabs to us but we were all familiar with those. He got the Frenchman to pull back the foreskin, which attracted another punch and insult as he revealed a cluster of cauliflower-shaped penile warts. Once he had filled the cavity from the cyst with a strip of lint soaked in Betadine, which would drain the infection from the hole and would have to be replaced each day, he injected Lignocaine into the young lad's bell-end. I inwardly winced as I saw the needle go in, but when he started to burn off the warts with a heated wire that resembled a soldering iron and the guy's bell-end was in flames, I had to clench my teeth. I was glad that I had kept my cock in my pants for the last few months.

The hospital was divided into different departments; the locals being separated from the white eyes (French) who generally had their own rooms. I had been on duty with Anna since ten o'clock the previous evening. It had been an annoying night as an old man who could hardly move rang his bell every two minutes, wanting to be moved from his left side to his right. As soon as we sat down again in the office the bell would ring and we would go to see him again. Eventually, Anna just tied the bell switch high out of his reach and we slept for a couple of hours on the chairs, leaving the old man to like it or lump it. We were in resuscitation where a few badly injured patients lay like breathing corpses on life-support machines.

I arrived at the still figure hidden beneath a sheet. I checked his chart and saw a red spot, which indicated that he was HIV-positive, so I knew to be careful not to get any blood on or in me. I had prepared six vacuumed test tubes and a needle in a silver tray for the morning blood sample.

'Shouldn't we wake him first?'

'Non, c'est ne pas la peine.' 'No, no point.'

I pulled the dark arm from under the sheet and slipped a tourniquet over the bicep to help find the vein. His skin was very black and his veins very small, so I slapped the crook of his arm a little to bring them out before cleaning the area with Betadine. Everything had to be immaculately clean in the hospital; we would avoid using our hands to apply a dressing, using sterile forceps instead. I stretched the skin and inserted the needle through his tough skin and into the vein.

'Aaaaaahhhhh gggrrraaaaah!'

He bolted up straight, making gurgling noises. I held on tight, holding the needle in while trying to keep dry from the spittle and blood. He had been shot in the head a few days previously. The bullet had tracked around his face removing his nose, part of his cheekbone and mouth. I could see through his nose to his back teeth and back out again through the gaping bleed hole in his cheek. While I concentrated on the needle Anna went bezerk:

'Ta gueule!' 'Shut your trap!'

She grabbed his head and violently forced it back on the pillow with her right arm. I looked at her, amazed at her manner.

'Ta gueule!' 'Ta gueule!' 'Putain!' 'Shut your gob!' 'Shut it!' 'Fucker!'

I looked at her in amazement, not expecting this type reaction from a French nurse. While she banged the guy's head on the pillow and slapped him, I extracted eight test tubes of blood.

Upstairs a young French lad sat upright reading a magazine. The big lad was full of muscles and obviously trying to impress the nurses. Anna was 32 and married to a Legion sergeant major. We informed the French regular soldier that we would be putting a needle into his arm. Nonchalantly he flopped out his arm while still reading his book.

I looked at Anna and knew exactly what she was thinking. I thought to myself, 'You wait! Big time it in front of us and we'll see how tough you are in a minute!' The nurse handed me the biggest needle she could find and gave me a knowing nod. I put a tourniquet on his big bicep and slapped a vein to make it rise. The needle went through his skin … No reaction. Right! I popped it through the vein and began to twist it around a bit. I looked up, satisfied to see his eyes wide open, hear him moaning and looking at his arm in horror! I pulled it out and with a new needle chose another vein.

'Not reading your magazine this time?'

I popped it in, taped it up and started 1 litre of saline dripping at ten drips a minute, before injecting antibiotics directly into the rubber nozzle of the catheter.

'Petit enculé!' 'Little arsefucker!' Anna said, as we closed the door behind us, pushing the trolley to the next room and consulting our list of jobs.

Patients were being prepared for their operations. Halfway down our list we had a local who was in to have his enormous haemorrhoids removed. Once again I was glad of a strong stomach, as I inserted a tube up his rectum and squeezed in a litre of warm soapy water from a rubber pouch. I pointed at him and laid down the rules.

'Do not let go! ... Hold it in for ten minutes.'

I held up my two hands and pointed to my watch and then to ten minutes later. I used my hands to express myself frequently. It became a habit when dealing with people who could not grasp the French language. Lads from the Far East had trouble with the language. We had a Japanese guy in the platoon who still could not understand a word after four years. He would not be promoted since he never passed the annual French assessments, which were a deciding factor on your future with the Legion.

Ten minutes later, when the poor patient's veins were popping out of his head, his teeth were clenched with concentration on not breaking my rules, and I thought he was going to burst a blood vessel, I passed him a bowl and pushed him onto the toilet. He needed to be clean inside and out. I then had the unpleasant task of shaving around his piles, which (in tradition of the phrase) did look like a bunch of grapes!

Meal times were exceptional. Suddenly a patient had more friends than he could handle, each one helping himself to his food. It became a mad house! We went into theatre to watch the survivors of a truck crash being put back together. It was a busy period in which I spent a lot of time suturing deep wounds and cuts. I watched as the surgeon removed a middle finger and neatly sutured a triangular piece of flesh in its place. It was an impressive technique. Anna picked it up and waved it, asking if anybody wanted a spare finger. We grinned and declined.

I was with Duval in the hospital. He had studied medicine for a couple of years before joining the Legion, so he had a huge advantage over us in the classroom. We had a couple of patients upstairs who had both been shot in the spine. From the waist down they had lost all feeling. Every few hours we would empty their catheters and every day I would insert a new one. Each patient had a buzzer for assistance. They would only realize they had emptied their bowels from the smell as they had lost all sensation in the lower part of their bodies. Every time, we would turn them over, clean them and change the sheets.

The buzzer rang and the room stank. We had a couple of hours before the shift ended, so we tied the buzzers out of reach and waited for the relief, two Polish lads on the course, to arrive. As we left we informed them that the buzzer for room 21 had just rung and walked off grinning to ourselves.

She came in around 12 o'clock with her brother. They were both badly burnt – she was almost dead. The brother was still conscious at the time and explained what had happened. She was a local girl and her parents had arranged for her to marry an older man, but she refused. For punishment her parents took her outside, doused her in petrol and lit a match. The rationale being that if she survived she would never marry anyone and if she didn't … well … let God sort her out! Her brother had tried to save her, but she died. My French buddy was quick to stuff her orifices with cotton wool before suturing them tight. This was to avoid making a mess in the hospital ward when her body relaxed. When the muscles relaxed everything would come gushing out on the floor.

One morning the man who lost his finger came back in with his hand bleeding from a wound in the palm. It was venous bleeding, and like a tap it steadily ran over his clothes. We took off the bandage and made him raise his arm to slow the flow of blood to the wound. The doctor arrived and began to rummage around the wound for the vein with a pair of forceps. Three of us held him down while he struggled and screamed, and Anna swore continuously at him to 'Shut up!'

Once I had finished my medics course I was invited to join CECAP as an instructor. It was a privileged invitation. I had made an impression on the previous course, and the officer in charge had requested that I join the 12-man team. I didn't really want to leave the combat company, but I had heard a rumour that since I was a corporal and a medic I might be needed to work in the medical centre in the main camp. I did not want to take the chance of ending the next year in the infirmary, so I packed my things and I got on the next truck to Arta Beach to meet the team; an officer, a sergent-chef, a couple of corporal-chefs and eight of us corporals. Instructing at CECAP seemed a better option.

This was a relaxed atmosphere. People were nice to us because they wanted favours. The senior officers would arrive at the centre and want a lift to an island or a diving trip, so they always tried to keep us happy. I spent the next few days learning how to pilot the zodiacs and rehearsed teaching the assault courses and rope work. I recited my medical lectures and sorted out the medical centre with the corporal-chef.

CECAP was miles from any services. Once a month a ship would arrive and we would roll out fire hoses to the tanker to pump fresh water into the tanks in the rear of the compound. Each week we drove a couple of hours back to the camp of the 13 DBLE at Djibouti to get diesel for the generators, fresh food and supplies.

It was another month before the next course would start. I started going out fishing with some of the lads. We would either drag a small lure behind the boat on the coral reef or take out the harpoons. Harpoon fishing was great fun but it could be dangerous. Sharks would be attracted to the blood and the injured fish that got away. We snorkelled for hours trying hard to get deeper to the big fish, which, once spiked, I would carry in a mesh bag on my waist.

The course arrived on the Friday evening and settled in for the night. They were a French army platoon from the 3rd Infantry Marines. I took them through their lessons, demonstrating the techniques for crossing all the obstacles during the day, and in the evenings taught them knots and the *tyroline simple*; things that I had learnt from my previous courses in France.

As a medic I also taught basic first aid and how to make improvised stretchers with scrap wood and bits of canvas, or a couple of combat jackets. When the soldiers weren't running around they explored the beach, which gave me plenty of work to do in the medical centre, as they continuously cut themselves on the coral or stood on black sea anemone. There was nothing I could do for this apart from soak their feet in vinegar, which would help the pain. The black needles were like very soft wooden splinters, which broke each time I tried to remove them with tweezers. From time to time the locals would arrive with their ailments, many of which were fictional: they simply wanted something; a bandage, some pills, anything. An old man arrived limping and complaining of back pain. I tried the usual tests, but it was hard to tell if there was a problem and even if there was, what could I do apart from give him an aspirin? So I sellotaped a Quinine tablet to his forehead, waved my arms around a bit saying in English:

'You are healed … You can now walk away!'

He stood in front of me absolutely motionless as I carried out the charade, taking the whole thing completely seriously. He thanked me for my witch doctoring and walked away without a limp. Once around the corner, Damien, a fellow instructor who was also on my promotions course, and I laughed our heads off. For sore feet and ankles I only gave aspirin to increase the circulation, as generally it was a ploy to get out of running around the assault courses. On one occasion a Japanese legionnaire came to me with blisters that I had never seen the likes of before or since. The entire surfaces of both feet were one large, deep blister. I drained them with a needle and left the thread in place to dry the cavity. Regardless of his blisters, he was told to continue. and spent the next few days running and marching in the desert, during which time he didn't complain once.

When the legionnaires came to do the course they would often bring their own dose of *Trobicine*, bought from the town for infections such as gonorrhoea. I would cure their stinging, dripping penis with the injection that they had bought to avoid going to the doctor.

It was good to be on the giving instead of receiving end. I treated the lads fairly, and always did exactly the same as them on the warm-ups as some instructors had done with me when I was on courses. On the final unarmed combat session, however, I went to town; shouting abuse in English to enhance the effect. I remembered running around and being shouted at in a language I could not understand when I first joined. I wanted them to know how it felt. They had not followed the same programme as the Legion. They hadn't been tied up or marched around for days on end. The Legion always had to make things as hard as they could to prove how tough they were.

As they punched my glove and kicked I could see the same hatred in their eyes that I'd had with my instructor. I was glad. It was an 'I went through it, so should you' philosophy. I realize now, years later, this doesn't always work. It felt good at the time and it was good for the training, and they may have benefited – they may have been tougher or harder fighters in the future. They would have been more aggressive and most probably one or two would develop a hate for the English that could manifest itself in years to come.

That evening I went for a few drinks with the course in the classroom and sang a few songs. They sang a song similar to a Legion song but with different lyrics, so I sang louder and harder to make my words heard. Most of the lads seemed fine, but I could feel the eyes burning into my back and see the stares of hate from one or two. I didn't care. In my Legion mind they were just French 'Slappies', a nickname for any soldier that was not a legionnaire, and were not fit to wipe my Legion butt! 'Fuck You!' My aggression and anger had reached a peak. I didn't care any more. Who gave a fuck anyway?

We had a continuous supply of cold Heineken from the cookhouse. This was ideal as I drank every night. The only other English speaker was Stan, a former RUC officer from Northern Ireland. He was the resident unarmed combat instructor. After visiting the local bar we went to the beach and finished off a bottle of whisky, and talked about the situation in Northern Ireland and his wife and kids. In the shadows to the rear a couple of Ethiopian girls waited hoping to be called over. They sat with us and told us how they used to think the legionnaires just got paid for doing nothing and drinking beer as that was all they saw of us in the city, but since they had been here they had seen us return from the marches, with a few days growth upon our chins and bloodshot eyes, desperate for a cold beer or soft drink, in the early hours of the morning. It is often the case, with many people who look on as outsiders, only seeing the time off and parties and never witnessing or experiencing what goes on when the Lrgion is away in the desert or on operations.

We toasted to the Legion and listened to Irish folk music while we watched the glowing red tracer from the bullets and explosions from the other side of the water. The Afar rebels were still fighting and most of the country had been out of bounds for a year now. We discussed what the diving would be like in the North when the war was over and the coral was virgin again. Stan was on leave but he chose to stay at Arta Beach to fish and spend some time out on the boats. He left with one of the Ethiopian girls in a Zodiac as the sun began to rise and would return a few days later. Fires were still burning and smoke drifted onto the hill on the other shore. Stan didn't take much with him – a few pots of coconut milk, some lemons, a fishing line, harpoon gear, some beer and a whore. He didn't need much else for leave in Africa. We often caught parrotfish on the reef, which we soaked in lemon juice for a day to 'cook' the flesh, and then soaked in coconut milk. Stan had a healthy diet of raw fish and beer for days on end, boating from island to island under the clear hot skies.

I discovered that the instructor that had beasted me at the end of my course had never done a commando course himself. We had a heated argument about this over a few beers one evening. I didn't respect him because I didn't think he had the right to teach if he had never been on the receiving end. We almost came to punches, but to solve the argument he challenged me to do the cable assault course right there and then at night and without safety. We drove up the wadi to the start point. Damius was half-French and half-Moroccan and we were good friends. He tried to talk us out of it, but eventually he agreed to time us each individually. The series of single and double cables stretched from rock to rock. The drop was about 100 feet, and you would be unlikely to survive if you fell.

He went off first and I started a couple of minutes later. The cables swung from side to side: below I could just see the edge of the rock face and the white letters of the Voix de L'inconscient. In the warm clear night, I could see him up front. I pushed hard. My lungs were screaming for air but I was slowly gaining. I was still drunk but in control enough to feel safe and confident. I ran across the three-cable bridge, putting each foot at a 90-degree angle to the cable to avoid slipping. One of the confidence tests is to make a metre-and-a-half jump from a steep cliff to a telegraph pole. At night this was daunting. But off I went and carried on, finishing with the abseil, facing down towards the ground Australian style, which helped me gain speed to the point that I was almost running. On the bottom we stopped the clock. I had just beaten him by seconds. I had to prove a point. We shook hands and never mentioned it again.

We had a mixture of animals in the centre. They were generally wild but we had tamed them. A grey and ginger cat weighed in at 14 kilograms and was an evil creature that acted as if it begrudged its weight. I tried to stroke it but it hissed and scratched my arm. I offered it a fresh live fish, which it ate it in two bites, before sloping off to the shade like an ungrateful child. Although hugely overweight it was fantastic at catching mice, which it would bring into the kitchen and feast upon.

We went fishing when we had time to ourselves, so generally we ate fresh fish each day. We would take it in turns to experiment in the kitchen with anything we could think to use. I began to create a batter flavoured with curry sauce in which I would dip morsels of red snapper before deep-frying them. This was always a favourite with the lads. But generally we lit the barbeque and toasted the fish over the flames or wrapped them in foil with lemon, tomato and garlic.

Small wild cats would scavenge the boat stores for food during the night. We often found their bodies around the camp. The four wild dogs had changed masters many times as instructors came and went but they were fantastic animals. Loyal to each other and to us in the centre – anything else was treated as prey. They hunted the cats as a pack, blocking the escape routes and channelling the poor beasts to a corner and ulti-mately death. They didn't eat their kill. They killed for pleasure or sport. A concept considered in human terms to be immoral.

The baboon was tied to the amphibious assault course, which was kept out of the water when not being used. The wives and girlfriends of the French forces stationed in Djibouti would sometimes stay in the chalets up the path, but the macaque would masturbate as they walked past on the beach, so he had to be castrated by one of the medics.

It was a crafty little baboon, and could untie any knot, so we were forced to attach the rope with bolts. Occasionally, it would escape and sneak back to us, playing a hide-and-seek game, but it always returned later. He had been domesticated. In the evenings we would occasionally take the baboon and dogs for a walk to the only bar in 30 miles. It was a large, quiet place a couple of hundred metres up the beach, and we were usually the only clients. The girls that ran it were Ethiopians who I had begun to know quite well. They were friendly girls who would make us Ethiopian coffee.

The monkey would stay high, clinging to the pillars, and at every opportune moment would scurry to the floor, quietly creeping behind an unsuspecting dog. The dog would yelp as the macaque yanked its testicles and jumped for the safety of height. They were amusing to watch. Every now and then we would allow the baboon to have a few beers with us. It was hilarious to see it squat on the bar and hold a bottle of Heineken between its small four-fingered paws. After a few beers it became either emotional or aggressive, very similar to a few humans that I knew. It would choose a person and cling to him all night. If anyone else approached it would bare back its teeth and screech. It had a ferocious bite, so I was frequently suturing the wounds it would make.

I had heard stories of baboons in Djibouti in their native habitat attacking villages and even raping women. I had seen them in the wadis when out on the field. As night fell they would gather in the low ground out of sight. On the highest point two adult males would sit all night and keep watch. When I used to mount the guard in Arta, a pack of baboons would hang around the barbed-wire perimeter fence. When the sun was hot and most of the lads had gone inside to avoid the heat, they would attack. Their target was always the cookhouse. We would shoo them off with baseball bats, and occasionally we would shoot them if they attacked. They were magnificent creatures, but also scarily intelligent and aggressive. When an adult male looked you in the eye you knew that behind its deep-brown, human-looking eyes it was assessing you, deciding if you were a threat. I can imagine them attacking an unarmed nomadic family in the mountains. Without weapons humans are easy prey. Back to basics and we are not king of the jungle.

After I had taught on a couple of courses I was given my first leave for 20 months. I was entitled to 20 days so I travelled to Djibouti with Stan. It was dark as we stopped for a beer in Oueah on the main road to Arta. The bar was opposite the camp in which the Legion Cavalry Company from the 13 DBLE was stationed. It was dark inside; an orange glow from a single hanging bulb allowed us to see our way to the bar. We had a choice of beverages – straight whisky or beer. We ordered both and sat down. The solitary table, floor and corners boasted an abundant insect life. Thousands of cockroaches crawled around our feet while little lizards crawled around the walls. The blades of the fan, yellow with dust, could hardly turn with the weak electrical current, which left the insects active in the heat.

I slapped a mosquito on my neck and turned to look out the back door. A French legionnaire on leave was sitting outside his house made of rocks. It looked like an igloo made of lava rock. A candle gave a warm glow, which cast flickering shadows of a niah stoking a fire. The legionnaire had finished his two years in Djibouti, gone to France and then returned back here to spend his leave living with his local girlfriend. I thought he was totally mad but he seemed happy, living in his house made of stones. All I wanted to do was get out of there. I'd had enough of the dirt, the heat and the sweat. We drank whisky for a couple of hours before Stan dropped me off in the main camp where I found my room in the Bordello.

The Bordello (a resident Legion brothel, which would only open in certain regiments overseas, the last one having closed down in Calvi around 1982) had just opened and for a few weeks hookers loitered around the bar looking for any drunk legionnaires for a bit of business, before the commanding officer's wife changed the rules. It would come and go depending on the officers in charge and their wives!

Duval was the duty medic so he had a couple beers before checking the blokes and whores for sexually transmitted diseases. I had a couple of bottles of Heineken before meeting Mac in town. We bought our usual bottle of gin and began to party. We messed about and I accidentally broke my nose. I could feel it flat across my face, pointing towards my ear. Mac put it right for me. I was too drunk to feel the pain. Isabelle was there so I took her to her friend's house and we made love while she wore my Legion shirt and képi. She used to get lifts from people to travel the 50 miles into the desert to visit me, but I heartlessly treated her like a quick shag: cuddles and compassion was something alien to me. I had the keys to the medical centre where we fucked on the same couch that I treated patients. She always wanted to stay but I used to leave her and drink beer with the boys. I wasn't interested in that. I just wanted to get rid of some pent-up tension before making a bit more. I returned to the Bordello and fell asleep to the sound of two Frenchmen sleeping with a couple of local whores in the room next door.

While I was on leave with Isabelle the 13 DBLE deployed to Somalia. I returned to camp to see if I could join them as most of the regiment had gone. Unfortunately, at least one medic was required to stay at CECAP and that was me. I was gutted but you cannot choose your operations. I hoped my time would come eventually. One day I wouldn't care for operations and would know that I should leave the military – but for the moment I hoped.

The good thing was that back in the commando centre we were now only four, the rest having deployed to Somalia, leaving the highest rank a corporal-chef. Each day we went either diving or fishing. I had scuba-dived for the first time when I was posted to CECAP. I put on a tank, which was held by a thin strap, a set of fins and a mask. This was all we required.

'Just remember ... Always breathe.' This seemed an obvious thing to do! Because the air pressure is doubled at ten metres below the surface, the air volume is halved. Consequently, a full lung of air at ten metres is the volume of two lungs on the surface. Hold your breath when ascending and you literally 'blow-up'!

With my two minutes of training complete, I descended to a depth of forty metres. I followed Damius along the drop-off. This was the point where the coral reef ended and the deep water started. It was the best place to fish and also the best place to see the life. I peeked into the holes and gaps between the living coral to see the creatures lurking. An inquisitive Murray eel poked its head out to look at us. We pointed, but not close enough for it to react or to cause it to bite. Stovacs nudged me, putting his hand on top of his head like a fin. Shark! It snaked past a few metres away. It wasn't interested in us, so we stopped still and watched in awe. I could hear my breathing long and clear through the mouthpiece. The air tasted of oil from the old compressor, which didn't seem too safe. I watched the bubbles from my mouthpiece rise and expand to the surface. Everything was somehow calmer down here. I still wasn't confident with being under the surface, since I didn't really know what I was doing. The first time I took off my mask underwater was at 30 metres when some French instructors from the city came to test us and issue us our dive passes.

The reef was alive and we always saw something new. The circular motion of a turtle's feet would catch our eye and I guiltily thought of the one we had eaten. The bright purple and immense size of the huge parrotfish made me think of fishing and pulling in a big one. Somehow over the past four years my thoughts had gone from adventure and experience to aggression and death; kill this, eat that. We stopped at three metres to allow the nitrogen our bodies had absorbed to release. We didn't want to get decompression sickness when we surfaced, as the nearest decompression centre was miles away in Djibouti city. The nitrogen could release into the joints and bloodstream, which was painful. Often when we pushed the depths to over 40 metres I would get aches and pains and feel very drained, but a few beers would soon make me forget.

I have since learnt to dive correctly and the way in which we dived in the Red Sea seems like madness now: at the time I would do anything and trust anyone. It would only be later when I reacted more with civilians and women that I would lose my trust; when I entered the world of chirpy sales pitches and slanderous gossip. The world of 'we'll save you money!'; 'I'll pay you'; 'I won't tell anybody'; 'I love you'; 'she did this ... he did that'. The world where people were more interested in what other people were doing and the slandering of celebrities than with getting on with their own lives.

While the rest of the men were in Somalia, we relaxed by the sea. I would get up at nine in the morning and swim for a while. Stovacs and I would go trawling for tuna and barracuda in the deep water. We had bought some strong fishing line, a wire trace and a couple of lures from the city, which we dragged behind the boat, and waited for the solid tug on the other end. They were strong large fish that would dive deep when hooked, so we didn't pull the fish to us; rather we pulled the boat to the fish, winding the line around a block of wood as we went. A strong, quick haul brought the creature flipping on the deck. Reactions had to be quick. I wore neoprene gloves to hold the slippery body and an Opinel penknife to force into the brain to kill it. The three-pronged hooks were a danger to the inflatable rubber Zodiacs. Occasionally, we would puncture a segment but it would always stay afloat, as it was divided into separate airtight compartments. We ate well. Trawling was ok, but harpooning was much more fun.

Over Christmas and New Year we drank champagne and ate foie gras (a French delicacy of pate made from the livers of specially fattened geese or duck), caviar and steak. One of the lads came from a very rich family who continuously sent him parcels of expensive goodies. I didn't like the champagne, preferring to drink a beer instead.

Stovacs and I left around midday. He had joined before the civil war in Yugoslavia and used to joke with the other 'Yugo', who was Croatian. Back home their cultures were at war but here they joked as friends.

I piloted the boat while he trawled until we reached our favourite place for harpoon fishing. Once kitted up I leant backwards and dropped into the water. I circled until I saw the reef and slowly finned my way, scanning for fish as I went. I spotted a large grouper and hyper-ventilated to trick my lungs into thinking I had more breath. One last breath before tipping forward and diving deep: everything slowed. Slow motion was the key to energy conservation and successful hunting. Sharp movements scared the fish. I held the harpoon close to my chest before straightening my arm and taking aim. I could hear the crack and swoosh as I released the harpoon. Bull's-eye! I pulled the struggling fish back and put in it in my net bag. I could feel that it was going to be a good day.

It was deep but I thought I would have a go. The huge parrotfish slowly skulked at around ten metres. My lungs were screaming, but I was determined to make a kill. The harpoon hit its hard skin. It wiggled for a bit but managed to get away. To my left I saw it and my heart froze. A white tip shark was a couple of metres away. It was about a metre and a half long and clearly excited by the prospect of an easy meal. I surfaced and watched as the shark pounded the reef in a frenzy, stirring up the silt and sand. I had heard of white tips attacking harpoon fishermen so I turned and swam in the opposite direction. Over my shoulder I wasn't prepared for the sight I saw. The shark had found me interesting and was inches from my fins! I could see its head and body snaking from side to side. 'Great!' I thought as I popped my head out of the water to see the boat a hundred metres away. I kicked harder and quicker to get away but I soon decided this would just excite it more, and anyway I was not going to out-swim a shark! Another glance and it was still there. 'Right.' I slowed down and thought to myself, 'Well, if it bites it bites – what can I do? I'll just ignore it and maybe it will go away.' The perfect solution to a problem that is out of your control! I didn't hear the crack on the water, but the next time I looked it had gone. Stovacs was behind me waving with a huge grin on his face:

'Putain! ... J'ai cru qu'il allait te bouffer!' 'Fuck! I thought it was going to eat you! ... I slapped the water and it swam off.' Stovacs was fearless. He was a fantastic harpoon man and always returned with the biggest and best catch of the day. But his catch was not for the sharks! We would sit around the barbeque and he would tell his stories about them.

'Well, there I was with two huge snappers in my bag.' He pointed to the sizzling fish on the barbeque. They were indeed fine fish. 'And then it came from the left ... a *requin* [shark]. I thought, "You are not having my catch," so I put my fish behind my back and held my harpoon like this.' He squatted and demonstrated, pointing his empty fist to the left. 'When suddenly from the right, another came. Putain! I fended them off with my harpoon while "finning" back to the beach ... There was no way they were taking my fish!' We laughed and called him a crazy bastard. He always told stories that would keep us on the edges of our seats.

I had been in the Legion for four years, and life was now beginning to feel good, although my mind was hardly in a fit shape to truly appreciate it. I drank every night: the heat, isolation from civilisation, the continuous hassle from the locals and the beastings, had all had their effects. I hadn't been able to phone home since I had been in the country, but I still wrote to one of my brothers, who would occasionally write back. I had completely stopped caring about anything but the Legion and training; apart from that the world did not affect me. I wasn't a part of it. I rarely sat and reflected upon life as I had previously. I had accepted things for the way they were and it was a good feeling. My blissful ignorance had brought me contentment. It was like being a small child. One day I'd sat in an English lesson at the age of 14 and looked about me at all the other kids, thought about my life, about my parents' divorce and about the children's home and foster parents and thought, 'Why me? What's it all about?' That day I'd started to reflect upon my life; too young to realize that 'it' wasn't anything to do with me. Too ignorant to realize that self-pity wouldn't help. It was as if that moment had never happened.

I was on duty, which just meant that I had to sleep next to the radio instead of in the room next door with the others. I hadn't drunk much as I was on duty. I lay on the camp bed and closed my eyes. I could feel my breath on my sweaty top lip. Even with the air-conditioning, the temperature still reached the early 30s. The others were fast asleep. I opened my eyes and saw the creature on the ceiling above me. It spanned eight inches. Its eight thin legs held the weight of its small body to the plaster. I had seen spiders similar to this when I was a child. I used to play table tennis with my brother in a large barn. In the corners lurked hundreds of spiders with spindly legs and small bodies. They were, however, only small – unlike this red liquorice creature hanging in front of me. I knew it wasn't real. Real spiders are not made of sweets! My hallucinations were strange. I knew they were not real, but I could see them plain and clear as if they were. I watched without fear. What wasn't there could not hurt me. The time to worry is when you can't tell the difference between your hallucinations and reality. Then again if you are that far gone then you don't feel the need to worry.

On another occasion, I had woken in the afternoon during the siesta. More spiders; this time hundreds of them were scaling the lockers next to my bed. I saw them, but again knew that they couldn't be real. Not real in our everyday sense. I was now desperate to get away from the heat and dust.

The next night I had a shock. I could feel a strange hand in my bed on my leg. I grabbed it and squeezed. The more I squeezed the more it squeezed back. I wrestled in the bed:

'Putain! Putain enculé!' 'Fuck. Fuck, arsefucker.' The others awoke and grabbed their baseball bats. We had an intruder. I wrestled him to the door crashing around the grey lockers. He was strong and would not let go. I had difficulty with the door so I knocked it with my shoulder to open it. From behind a light shone through the cracks. Looking down I was holding my left hand with my right. No intruder. There was a commotion in the dark behind me.

'Putain! ... Il est où cet enculé?' 'Fuck! Where is the arsefucker?'

'Ça va ...Ça va.' I answered. 'It was nothing ... I fell asleep on my hand!'

We laughed and went back to sleep.

*

Mac returned from Somalia so I joined him in town for a drink:

'You didn't miss anything! It was crap!'

'We were next to the yanks! They had the lot ... showers ... cinema ... burger vans ... you name it.' The Legion was on the floor in tents nearby. Paddy had found a human head, so they put it as a centrepiece on the table. I looked at the photographs with interest. Mac explained a little more:

'This missionary turned up ... Irish woman in her sixties – stupid bitch! She slagged us off for three days, blaming us soldiers for the situation in the country.'

'Stupid bitch!' I agreed. 'She needs to get a grip on what is happening.'

'So anyway ... we tried to persuade her not to go up to the village ... we told her they would kill her! ... But, oh no! ...We were the cause of all wars, blah, blah, blah.'

I nodded and had a good swig of gin. A niah was trying to attract our attention by dancing in front of us; her light see-through dress showing a fine, fit figure, but it was too late for that. I was not interested. I was only interested in Mac's story and more alcohol.

'Dégage!' 'Bugger off!' She turned away saying something about us being *méchant* (nasty), and we were. We carried on chatting.

'So eventually we let her go ... We tried to warn her, but she ignored us. So she came back three days later ...' Mac held his arms out as if he were carrying heavy shopping. 'In four bin liners ... she had been raped and chopped up ... serve the stupid bitch right!' I shook my head in agreement and disbelief.

'People just don't learn … life is cheap, fucking cheap!'

We changed the subject and went to see the girls. I could hear glasses smashing downstairs as Mac fucked Marie-Clare on the bar that she owned, while I was upstairs with Isabelle on the restaurant tables. We didn't mind. If we could we would have swapped.

I was leaving soon. I needed to get back. I'd had enough of the heat, the dirt and the desert and I vowed never to return. I had another week's leave before I left. I had bought some civilian clothes and was on my way out when I heard a shot. There was a bit of commotion. I ignored it and carried on to the town. I later discovered that one of the French sergeant majors had shot himself in the head when he discovered that his wife had been having an affair with their 'boy'. Boys were employed by the white eyes to clean and cook. I didn't know him. 'Idiot,' I thought. 'You should have shot your wife and the boy first!'

Each time a Brit finished his two-year tour it was a tradition that we had a drink and he signed the Union Jack that had been passed from person to person as they left. We bought a few bottles of spirits and stacked up the cases of beer. They were good nights. There was usually a fight and a bit of blood would be spilt. This was acceptable. Paddy and Brown had a fight on my leaving do. Brown left with a large cut to his head. We went to look for him and found him unconscious in the dust. We dragged him to the medical centre and he was lucky to survive. He was immediately taken to hospital to have his blood replaced.

The next day I made sure I woke. I gave the flag to

Mac and said goodbye. I shook hands with everyone. Damius slapped me on the shoulder:

'Vas y!' 'Go on!'

I left on the coach to the airport, happy to leave and yet sad to leave my friends. Some I would never see again.

.... CHAPTER 12

I was glad to leave Africa and impatient to get back to France. I was entitled to two-and-a-half months of well-earned leave. The flight seemed to last days although it was only eight hours: all that time away and yet only eight hours. But the plane was the coolest and cleanest place I'd been for two years. I couldn't believe I was on my way. Two years away with the Legion in the desert without a single phone call is a long time. I needed to get back and see people again.

I spent another week in Aubagne, waiting impatiently for my AIDS test to come back clear, picked up crabs from the bedding, which had almost become a tradition in itself, and finally went on leave after seeing the doctor, who dropped my psycho/mental level by two points. After a two-year posting in the desert we were considered to be a little unstable for a while. I caught the overnight train to Paris and slept on a small bed in a cabin. The fare was cheap as I received 75 percent discount with my French military ID card. The next day I found a nice hotel, walked around Châtelet les Halles and purchased some civilian clothes before sitting in the 'James Joyce' (an Irish pub), to contemplate how I would spend my leave. I had sent home about £7,000 over the past two years, which I thought would last me for the ten-week summer holidays. I noticed a nice pale Irish girl behind the bar and after a few beers we started chatting. She had long blonde hair, a soft peachy complexion and grey eyes. After two years I was glad to chat to a pretty face, knowing that later it would not try to rifle through my pockets or coerce my drunken body into sexual intercourse for 15 quid.

In the evenings I lost track of time. For two years it had become dark at six o'clock and suddenly I would look at my watch and realize in was 11 o'clock on a summer evening, and think I was late for appel! I left my bags of new clothes behind the bar before heading off to 'La Scala'. The cars rushed past at lightening speeds and people were everywhere. I wasn't used to this noise; the hundreds of rushing cars, the bright lights and sparkling shop displays. I hadn't seen a traffic light or zebra crossing for two years. I wasn't excited like the first time. I was confused. Who were all these people? What did they do? I looked at the people dancing and felt alienated from them. It was going to be a long time before I would be able to tolerate society again. I considered the men who were not military to be worthless and the women had only one purpose. Unless a man was a soldier then as far as I was concerned he was not a man. At the time I was so engrossed with being a legionnaire that I hadn't actually considered civilians. The Legion was self-contained: we had our own cooks, clerks, cleaners, bar-staff, builders and plumbers and we didn't need anyone else. The indoctrination of the past four years had worked, and I was now a fascist. I thought the world should be ruled by the military. The military was all there was. Like a sponge I soaked it up.

I drank whisky and found an accommodating French girl to sleep with. I didn't remember her name and I am sure she doesn't remember mine. It wasn't important. I felt nothing in the morning. I just put my clothes on, said au revoir and returned to the 'James Joyce' to get my bag.

I had acquired a new passport by telling the passport office that I had lost my old one. On the trains home I looked with amazement. Everything was green. It was lush and cool and the air smelt fresh. I had trouble adapting to the crowds in the cities and crossing roads became a mission in itself. So many cars – so fast – so many people. What was going on? It seemed strange to be back, as if I had just walked back into a dream that I had long ago. The silence of the desert, the dingy bars, the once strange but now familiar smells and sounds of Africa were still fresh in my mind. As I walked through the streets I noticed everything, every window, every flash of skirt or leg, every smell and each little noise. I was happy to be back but lost in a strange world. This madness of the city was too much.

I had changed so much during the past four years. It amazed me how the whole thing worked. I would stand in a queue and watch a spotty youth, laboriously slowly, punch numbers into a machine. I thought, 'Hurry up! Why are you so slow?' I walked around the streets dodging between people: 'Come on, get out of the way!' An old lady shook a moneybox at me. I looked on the side at the Oxfam sticker. She began to talk to me but I wasn't listening. I was thinking about the woman washing her feet while a man died of thirst metres away. I thought of the young girl who had been burnt to death by her parents. I thought of the missionary being raped and chopped up with machetes. I looked at the old lady and her tin and felt nothing. I shut my eyes, turned my head and walked away. That was in 1993.

I visited my brothers who were both living in Hereford. I was so jubilant at being back in England that I frequented the bars and clubs each night. It was good to go for a few beers with my brother, but something was missing. I missed the Legion and my friends. I thought about what decision I would have made if I had been given the choice. Kill one of my brothers or one of my mates. I reflected upon the blood link. What made a family a family? Kids would grow up together and that would create the bond, just as I had grown with the Legion and a bond had been formed. Blood didn't matter. The simple fact that two people share the same blood didn't mean that they were family. If we traced our bloodline back far enough we would probably find that most of us are related. We are all blood brothers but true brothers don't need blood to bond them.

I soon became restless with the small town of Hereford, so I caught the train to Ipswich to visit my mother. I hadn't seen her for three years. I had sent her some photographs, but we didn't have a lot of contact. When my parents divorced I was about four years old, and we were living in a council house on the outskirts of

Norwich. Throughout my childhood I would see my mother every two or three years for a few days. As an adult she was more like a stranger. How could I relate to her when we didn't have a history together? She lived with a West Indian who worked nights. I rarely saw him when I visited. He was either in bed or working. Mum had not worked in years.

'I wuz wurkin in that chicken factry ... that wuz a grate job that but it made me 'ands sor! That wuz a grate job that!'

My mother had never been abroad and had rarely left Norfolk or Suffolk. She was a country woman who didn't care for politics or the rest of the world. On her side of the family the history stretched back to a small village in Norfolk and a heritage of servitude for the manors. On my father's side I had the tough resilience of Yorkshire coalminers. My grandfather had died in the mines, and my father worked in them as a child.

I didn't know too much about my family. I discovered as an adult that I had nine half-sisters and a half-brother. I had never met them and I didn't wish to. Blood doesn't always make family: I had my family in the Legion and they would die next to me. We would die together. The bond was strong, weakened only with age and separation just like a regular family.

I sat down on the scruffy sofa and looked at my mother. She was still a good-looking woman although now slightly plumper. She went to the microwave and pulled out a bottle of Vodka. She always had her little caches around the house. Each time I visited she would say that she had not been drinking and then send me

down the shop for four cans of Special Brew. I opened a
beer and we struggled to have a conversation:

'So wair you been? Arfrica?'

'Yeah, Djibouti.'

'Whairs thart then? Oi dunno much abart the world.'

'It's where the Indian Ocean meets the Red Sea,
between Ethiopia and Somalia.'

'Oh.' I sipped the treacle-thick Special Brew during
the awkward silence that followed. I knew she hadn't
understood where it was.

'Oi like your photos ... is that you parachuting?'

'Yeah ... in Calvi.'

'Whairs thart then?'

'France.'

'Oh I know that ... snails an all that.' She cackled to
herself. Another pause and a couple of sips of treacle.

'Oi dunt know 'baut that Samford ... e never gets out
of bed ... e's got loads of money but e just saves it an
never goes out or spends anything.'

'Yeah ... I'm going out mum.'

I had a shower. She made me a burnt burger and some
greasy chips. I ate most of it to be polite. I never stayed
for long. I walked to the rail station and had a pint in the
local bar, which was still quiet at eight o'clock. Maybe it
would get busy later. I asked the barmaid, to find out.
Barmaids were always my first choice when chatting up
girls. I have probably slept with more barmaids than
anyone else. I looked around for women but it was early.
A couple of hours later I went to find my mother again. I
found her in an old man's house, which smelt of stale
biscuits. I could remember staying there as a child

during a week's school holiday. Samford had thrown us out. My mother held the door shut to stop us kids getting in while he threw plates at her. He was a bit more active then. My older brothers were around 13 or 14 at the time. They were shouting and trying to get in. We went to this biscuit-smelling house and slept on lumpy mattresses that smelt of dogs. The old West Indian who owned it was nice enough.

As I walked through the door a man jumped out of the window. I saw him run and climb over the fence at the rear of the garden. A few old West Indian men were drinking with my mother. She cackled.

'You see that silly bugger ... oi told im that you was my son from the Foren Legun just back from Aafrica an you would cut a nigger's ead off loik you wuz toppin a carrart!'

I laughed. I hadn't a quarrel with anyone. I wasn't a racist although I worked with plenty, many of who were my great friends. I sat and had a whisky. They carried on chatting and drinking.

'I remember you when you were a little boy ... He's a man now, Peggy!' I sat silent for a while and wished I were somewhere else. I liked to visit my mother, but I could never stay for long. I don't think I have ever stayed longer than one night. I became bored and the conversation was difficult.

The next morning I took the train to London and caught a plane to Spain to visit my father. My father had remarried a primary school teacher and they had been living near Malaga on the Costa del Sol since the early eighties. I walked past the rundown council estate off the beaten track away from tourists' eyes and followed the path up the narrow spur. The villa was a couple of miles inland. I had my bag slung over my shoulder and a bottle of water in my hand. The Spanish sun was warm and I soon began to work up a sweat, which smelt of beer from the previous night. I remembered the track from six years previously. I used to walk down it to the beach and try my Spanish with the locals. They tended to treat you differently if you at least made an attempt to speak their language. I always thought the English were ignorant to live somewhere and not even make the effort to learn the language. My father had been there for ten years and yet his Spanish was still broken and amateur. He would add English words in a Spanish accent to make up the sentences. But it was quite amusing to hear.

'Uno sacko de cemento blanco por favor, you know like,' in a broad Yorkshire accent.

The house was quiet. I knocked again but still silence. The door opened when I tried the handle. I was beginning to wonder if he had moved on, but once inside the familiar items confirmed his presence. The onyx ashtrays that he considered to be worth a fortune, the rug no one was allowed to step on and the electric organ with which he played the longest Spanish eyes ever known. A note would last at least a minute before a quick succession of notes close together, before another minute of anticipation. I used to wonder how long it would take before he would change notes. I would wait … now! No, not yet. I saw the van through the kitchen and remembered the trip from England to Nerja in 1987. We had caught the ferry from Plymouth to Santander. It was winter and a force 10 gale was blowing across the Bay of Biscay. My father had spent some time sailing and travelling.

'You'll get used to it, Son. The first time I crossed the Bay of Biscay was in a flat-bottomed tug. That was in 1955 ... you know like.' He had never lost his broad Yorkshire drawl. I felt green with seasickness while I looked at his flowing black hair tinted with grey and his blues eyes. I had found my father alone in the centre of the restaurant. The ferry rocked and chairs were strewn across the deck. The staff had all gone to bed. The passengers had all gone to bed. The only person well enough to sit and drink tea was my dad. He had positioned his table and chair in the centre. His, for some reason, was the only table and chair still upright. The rest had been thrown to the edge of the room in messy piles. I told him I was going back to bed. I felt ill. 'You'll get used to it, Son.'

I heard my dad return an hour later as I could not sleep. I listened to the waves smash against the steel walls and tried to think of anything that didn't rock, but all that came to mind were grandfather clocks and park swings. He came in, lay down for a minute before getting up and retching into the toilet – *You'll get used to it, Son?* I grinned to myself.

'Even I can be sick from time to time, Son.'

I walked across the tiled floor. Inside it was cool. I could hear a television and soon found a room that had not existed before.

'All right, Son. Put the kettle on, lad.' I hadn't seen him for five years and he acted like I had been in the next room all along. It was hard to excite my father. I found the tea and brought it in. We sat and looked over the Mediterranean Sea. Shep, his sheepdog, came in and sat beside him, looking at me strangely as if trying to remember where he had seen me before. He was old now and the grey around his ears matched my father's.

We were silent for a little while. His skin was dark and hard from the 20 years he had spent working in the Middle East, mostly in the desert in Muslim countries away from the temptation of alcohol. His curved back cuddled his frame, slight with age. He always wore a pair of light slacks stained with paint and grease, desert boots, a pale shirt with a large collar and a straw hat. The veins on his arms bulged out like lugworms crawling along his skin. He was deathly thin.

'You know, Son ... I'm trained to kill too, you know like.'

'Oh yeah, Dad. What were you in?'

'They call it the Royal Corps of Transport now, you know like.' I thought back to his stories of when he was a conscript in the fifties. He used to laugh as he talked about driving dead bodies around in Egypt and how his local co-driver was convinced that they were still alive. As he laughed he leant his head forward, bobbing it up and down and making a half-whistling sound: 'sheeesh, sheesh, sheesh.'

Dad was thrown out after about a year for selling the red diesel to the locals. He always had a couple of tricks to make a little cash. I remember when I was about 15 years old and he used to take me out of school to work with him on his various projects. We went to a car

auction and he showed me how to put little bits of paper
in the rubber spark-plug sockets so that they wouldn't
conduct and the car didn't start. A car that was pushed
onto the stand would not fetch a great deal of cash, but
afterwards my father would remove the paper and drive
away!

I didn't really have much to say to him. We were
worlds apart, forty years between us. I stayed for a
couple of days but I soon grew impatient, so I went to
Torre del Mar to party. This was a tourist town on the
coast. You could find real Spain here. It was generally an
area for Spanish tourists; without the crowds of overweight Germans and fighting English clubbers. As with
most European countries there was very little point in
going out before midnight, so I went to the fish bars to
sample the fresh catch. I ordered some fried calamari
and a crab and sat next to an elderly Spanish lady. She
was surprised to hear that I was English and spoke a
little Spanish.

My Spanish was limited but enough to make friends
and chat. The bars were small and soon I became a bit of
a novelty as the English tourist. I was the only one. The
atmosphere was great. There were no hefty doormen or
dress codes. I simply mingled from one small bar to the
next. The girls and barmen would dance on the tables and
give me free shots. I spent a week there before moving to
the touristy side of Torremolinos. Torremolinos boasted
an active nightlife and a variety of lovely holidaying ladies
who were more than willing to share a night or two with
a lying Legion bricklayer. I had been on leave for six
weeks, so I returned to Paris to meet some old friends

and crawl the many Irish Bars. There were around 26 in Paris at the time. I would always meet some legionnaires in 'La Scala' or the 'James Joyce'.

I met Mac who had just arrived from Djibouti and we returned to England. We drank in the local bars around Hereford and spoke to some of the British Army guys there. Sometimes I would find myself asking for words in English that I had forgotten. Looking back it seems incredible that I could begin to lose my native tongue, but I was thinking and dreaming in French or Spanish and sometimes the English was just missing. Mac and I discovered we had a new trait: when speaking English with a group, we would use French words and slang quite a bit, which would eventually turn to fluent French. We would change from one language to the other without realizing, and wonder why the group was not joining in!

It was during a night out with my brother that the seriousness of my father's illness came to light. He had been diagnosed with cancer of the oesophagus, and the Spanish doctors had given him six months to live. It was unlikely that I would see him again unless I returned to Spain immediately. I found him in a hospital in a room on his own. He had drips in both arms and an oxygen mask over his mouth.

It reminded me of when I was a child in the early eighties and used to visit him in the psychiatric ward after he'd lapsed into a drinking binge for a week or two. I would play table tennis or watch television on the black and white portable with the 'nutters' (who were only nuts to everybody else but totally sane to themselves, which I thought was fine). Prior to one such visit to the psychiatric hospital, I'd sat by his bed at home when he was drunk and he gave me £5 for a bottle of whisky. I spent it down the local snooker hall with my school friends. When I returned much later he had drunk the last of his aftershave.

This time, I sat down lost for words and looked at his frail frame. What do you say to your dying father? What last words could we say to each other?

'All right, Son. The bloody nurses in here are useless. All I want is a drink of water.' I brought back a bottle from the cafeteria and a Coke for myself. His wife was back in England for a while as were my brothers.

'So how long are you going to be in here for then, Dad?'

'Oh I don't know, Son … they can't speak a bloody word of English!'

He had small white traces of spittle on the edges of his mouth and his eyes looked sad. He didn't cry or make a scene. We just sat together in silence and I felt numb. I thought about life and death. Life was cheap. It was death that cost. I was hardened to the reality of it all. Why get too upset? It happens to us all. Accept it before it happens and it doesn't hurt so much. The dead don't mourn, only the living. The dead aren't getting upset and wailing and blaming the world for what they deep down already know. I checked my watch. I had to catch a plane to Marseille.

'I've got go now, Dad.'

'All right, Son … I'll see you soon then.' He always had hope and never gave up. He always had something to do the next day, always a reason to get up in the morning. 'I can't be in here long, Son. I've got to build that wall out the back.'

'Yeah, Dad … the wall … Well, I'll see ya then, Dad.'

'Yeah, see you, Son, you know like.' I shook his hand and turned away. That was the last time I was going to see him. I sat on the bus back to Malaga and thought about him lying there alone.

.... CHAPTER 13

I spent a couple of days in Marseille before returning to Aubagne for my next posting. I knew the town quite well, often meeting legionnaires down the *vieux port* where the bars were small and frequented by dark-haired girls. This was the south where many of the people had Hispanic features. In one of the bars I met Stovacs again. He had returned to France from Djibouti a couple of months before me and had been posted to the 1eme RE, which suited him fine. It was a relaxed way of life, and he still managed to deploy on operations in the Balkans, which was great for him as he spoke the language and knew the people.

He leant forward, his eyes lighting up with a new story. His large frame cast a shadow on the white plastic table.

'Putain! Tu vois ma nouvelle bagnole!' 'Fuck! Do you see my new car!'

'Nice, Stovacs. Where did you get it?'

'Ahh, this is a good one … I arranged a game of cards with the Arabs down here.' He looked over his shoulder to make sure no one was listening and got closer, his dark eyes narrowing. 'I didn't want to go alone, so I took Mr Beretta [his 9-millimetre pistol] and one of the lads with me. We were both tooled up, just in case ... you know these Arabs!' Stovacs was good at cards. He was a bit of a schemer. He could talk a night on the town or a packet of cigarettes from a nun, if he wanted! 'So we're in the bar, and there are all these Arabs around the table and in the shadows ... they are all carrying weapons. The bar is behind the Rue de la Cannebière ... you know the ones where you have to watch your back?'

I knew where he meant as I'd been there late at night a few times with a couple of local girls. The bars were always very small and the girls' busts were pushed up by an array of red or silver silk, gold sequinned material or black PVC. They had high heels and short dresses. I looked into their eyes and the younger ones seemed so innocent underneath their red eyelids, blue eyeliner and plastered foundation. And the older ones just looked bored. Their lips were always a full rosy red, but they spoke to us and didn't try to force us into anything. They were my friends, and the Legion's friends. Often I would meet a girl who knew people from Calvi or Djibouti. They knew all the legionnaires. We were good customers, never greedy and forever generous. I once bought a drink for a couple of girls that cost me 50 quid. I knew it was just a *bar à pute* (a whore bar), but Marseille had many late clubs that were always private and difficult to get in with a shaved head, so the legionnaires hung around the small dingy bars in which the hookers loitered outside in hope for a drunken pay packet.

'Poker! ... There is only me and this "gringo".' He always referred to strangers as gringos. 'We had six bricks on the table [£6,000], and this gringo had run out of cash. I checked my mate and I knew he was ready for it to kick off. Gringo bet his car. I knew he was bluffing so I saw him and put my hand on Mr B ... just in case.' He patted the front of his trousers to demonstrate where he kept his pistol; he always had it with him.

'He had three sixes but I had three kings! We made a quick exit with the keys and cash!' He laughed and slapped me on the shoulder. I grinned back. We had another couple of beers before he drove us in his new car at 140 mph to Nice, where we met his girlfriend and drank to the early hours of the morning. Stovacs invited me back to his girlfriend's place, but I declined, to look for whores in my drunken stupor. I found a road on which the girls still loitered late at night. After a few cold-shouldered responses, I only realized the truth when the largely built Tahitian informed me.

'Il y a que des mecs ici.' 'There are only blokes here.'

I opened my eyes enough to focus and looked at his stubble pushing through smudged lipstick and foundation. These were truly the most unfortunate men to become transvestites, cursed with the stocky manly build of the pacific islanders. I looked around me at the others and realized that my task was fruitless. The hairy legs shoulder length apart and the tight thick calf muscles didn't do it for me. A pretty French lady in her thirties slowly drove past inspecting the wares, and I silently wished she would stop and pick me up. I left and slept on a bench by the beach until the bars opened, where I had a beer before returning to Aubagne to catch crabs again and discover where my next posting or regiment was to be.

The next day I went to see the colonel, who offered me a career in the Legion. I declined the invitation of an unarmed combat instructor's course and a promotion to sergeant, preferring to ensure my return to the 2nd REP to see how things went there. Once you became a senior NCO in the Legion you lost your choice for postings, which meant that I risked being sent to a regiment in which I had no interest. I was only interested in returning to the 2eme REP, riding in a tank or armoured vehicle didn't interest me. I had only eight month left, so unless I signed on for another couple of years I could not be posted back to Africa or overseas. I hadn't planned on staying for longer than five years. However, I was later tempted when I realized life could be quite relaxed and was easier after the first five years was over. I met Lepin in the foyer. I remembered him beating Kader for being a minger when I was still a young legionnaire. He had just returned from two years in French Guyana. He had had a similar time to me, being promoted and then employed as an instructor in the commando centre there. He had chosen to stay and become a sergeant. I always thought he would.

I returned to Calvi and met my old friends. Once the parachute training had finished I was sent to the sniper platoon in the Fourth Company where I met the other NCOs and bought a welcoming case of beer for each room.

It was still summer. The tourists filled the beaches and the town boasted a selection of girls. I went to the 'Bar Select' and drank with the patron and his wife, who I had become friends with previously. I phoned him a few years later and we chatted: I was happy to know that he still remembered me and my exploits in the town. We played dice during the week for rounds of drinks. I was always very lucky; drinking a BMW (triple: Baileys, Malibu and Whisky) for every beer that I bought him if I lost. I knew many people in the town who frequented the bars or worked in them.

The Fourth Company was the most relaxed in the regiment. In the mornings we didn't get up at 05.30 to parade outside at 6 am; instead we stayed in bed and the duty corporal did a head count. It was the same for the evenings. It was this relaxed atmosphere that resulted in a better morale and therefore better-motivated soldiers. I thought about the First Company over four years previously, when I would be stood outside in the winter at five in the morning, fully dressed in parade uniform for the usual Saturday regimental parade. At six I would hear the Second Company whistle the wake-up call, and at 06.30 I would hear the Fourth Company whistle theirs. I could never understand why we had to get up so early to hang around.

I was enjoying myself with the sniper platoon. Occasionally I was duty NCO, which meant that I had to run the training, write the orders, do the roll-calls and organize the *corvées* (duties). It would be a busy week.

I stood to attention to the right of the platoon, and as the sergeant approached I barked out the orders.

'Section … Garde à vous!' 'Section … Attention!' It was barked as a single word and if I didn't hear a sharp single smack of palms on thighs I would repeat it.

'Troisième section rassemble … Dans les rangs, 33 caporals, première classes et légionnaires, deux en stages, un manquant, un a l'infirmerie, à vos ordres, sergent!' 'Third section assembled ... In the ranks 33 corporals, first classes and legionnaires, two on courses, one missing, one in the infirmary, at your orders, sergeant!' The last word was always an octave higher and louder than the rest. The missing man was a former British para, and yet another deserter.

At times I was duty company corporal and I would do the roll-calls, supervise the chores and march the hundred men, singing, to the Ordinaire. As I started the pace, asked for one of the lads to sing the first few words of the song to get the tone, say *trois quatre*, three four, and listened to the harmonious sound of the lads singing, I realized that I had come a long way. I had left the young lad in St Tropez far behind. I had calmed down a little with my leave, but Africa was still fresh in my mind and it would be a long time before I truly returned to 'normality'. I had seen many people desert, but I had stayed and would now reap the benefits. I had paid my way with sweat and determination to an easier life.

I did the commando course again. This time it was not as intense after being combined with a demolitions course. So instead of marching and running around in our spare time, we sat in lessons in the evening with calculators and formulae working out the required amount of plastic explosive to destroy a bridge or electricity pylon. Sabotage was the bread and butter of the Fourth Company. We spent a fair amount of time on the ranges destroying trees and old vehicle hulls. We would calculate each charge with exactly the required amount of explosive for the task.

*

The infiltration marches were long, and we did not want to carry more than we needed. The charges would be shaped to give maximum damage. Explosives invert their power; so to create a piercing charge we would construct a cone shape. This would mean that the massive expansion of gases would concentrate away from the base of the cone. A good technique is to wrap detonating cord around a full water bottle. Three layers are enough. This creates the same effect as the cone, but this time using the water to enhance the power. The water increases the power of the charge. We spent the evenings making homemade explosive with sugar, ammonia and other ingredients that you could buy in any hardware store.

The techniques to cause damage are plentiful. A simple grenade with the fly-off lever held tightly in place with a rubber band becomes a time bomb. We would remove the pin and drop it into the petrol tank of a vehicle. The time that it takes the rubber band to melt would allow the lever to fly and the grenade to detonate, enabling us to leave the target area. I collected my third commando badge and the demolitions one a couple of weeks later when we returned to camp to finish off the training.

We spent the remainder of the time jumping and doing exercises. We had recently received the new Minimi, a 5.56 light machine-gun, which was ideal for the infantry patrolling that we did. It could fire belts of 50 rounds or magazines of 30 up to 600 metres. It was good to have the same calibre rounds as the rifles, as we could distribute the rounds when needed and we didn't need to carry extra 7.5-millimetre belts. We had two Minimis in each combat group combined with a sniper and the 89-millimetre anti-tank rocket launcher (LRAC), which could be reloaded to fire rocket after rocket. Each rocket could penetrate 400 millimetres of armour or 1,000 millimetres of concrete to a range of 400 metres. To support this fire power we had a couple of corporals, a sergeant and four riflemen armed with the Famas, which could also fire anti-tank or anti-personnel grenades up to 100 metres from the shoulder. Or if you placed the rifle butt on the ground and used it like a mortar it could launch a grenade to 380 metres. To help out we also had a sniper with each group. It was a formidable amount of fighting firepower.

I had learnt about the Barrret 12.7-millimetre sniper rifle, which the section had had for the past two years, in the 13 DBLE. It was designed to shoot vehicles or equipment at long range, but some of our better shots could hit an oil drum a 2,000 metres. We had nine for the platoon. This long, heavy sniper rifle was used in the conventional three-man sniper teams: the 'Barret man', and two 7.62-millimetre FRF2 men. The Barret was stripped down and split between the group because it was so heavy.

On exercises the sniper platoon would sometimes be deployed in ten three-man teams to probe forward and if necessary disrupt the enemy's movements. We would also do *jolonage*. This was a route recce to allow the rest of the company to advance quicker to the target, which would usually be a sabotage task as two of the other platoons were demolitions. We would split the platoon into 20 to 30 guides, each with a leg of a couple of kilometres to memorize. As the company arrived we would stop them and request the password. Once contact was made the guide would join the rear of the snake and the next guide would lead to the next and so on.

Christmas was approaching. We soon cleared out one of the rooms in the platoon and made a bar. The last one that I helped build was in the 13 DBLE. It was outside and made of sandbags and camouflage netting. This time we constructed a Hawaii effect. We painted scenes of golden beaches and palm trees on the walls. The bar was made of wooden logs behind which an array of spirits and beer pumps rented from the town helped to create the effect. A couple of bright orange lamps tactically positioned created a warm feeling over the sand that we had collected from the beach, which lay a couple of inches thick on the floor. There were six companies in the regiment, each with at least 5 platoons, which made a total of at least 30 bars on the camp, each one with its own theme. I didn't help make the crèches, which each section made and competed for the best one. I wasn't interested. How can you become a cold-hearted killer and still have the hypocrisy to be religious? Thou shalt not kill? It just didn't make sense to me!

There were many talented musicians and live music was to be found occasionally around the camp. We had a couple of Hungarians in our platoon so, for Christmas, goulash, a Hungarian meat stew with dumplings, was on the menu. For the next two weeks we would run each morning before starting the daily drinking binge. Work would have to wait. I visited all the bars and sampled the array of foreign home cooked foods. It was a great atmosphere; a time to relax, catch up with the chat and old friends from the other companies. We were never allowed leave at Christmas. Christmas had to be spent with the family – the Legion. Some of the senior lads who had leave entitlement went home for New Year but I always stayed.

On Christmas Eve we went to the Ordinaire for a company party. We had built a stage and each platoon had organized some kind of entertainment. We had rehearsed a 'sketch' consisting of a couple of lads dressed as women who would fight to the theme music of *Rocky*. There were some good laughs, bands and comedians. We drank wine and champagne while eating lobster and exotic food. The white tablecloths were soon stained with the red and white wine made by the Anciens in the retirement home in Poloubier. Eventually it would be time to collect our Christmas present from the Legion. We knew what we would be getting as we had been given a choice from a few items. I chose a Gerber penknife from the array of pocket translators, Dictaphones or Transistor Radios. The captain called out my name and I went forward, saluted and received my final Christmas gift from the Legion. Five months later I would be leaving.

We spent the weekends drinking. On Saturday afternoon we would go mad, drinking and smashing the bottles on the bedroom floor among the sodden porn magazines. I had calmed down a little bit after returning from Africa: I no longer hallucinated but I still had little time for civilians. As I arrived at the end of my contract and frequented the town more often, I still went wild in town, drank copious amounts of beer, ran over cars, climbed streetlights and generally made a fool of myself. I had got into the habit of opening my beers with anything that was to hand; usually a quick swipe along the join of the bottle with a penknife, which would send the bottle top attached with the glass across the room. Occasionally, a swipe with a frying pan would do the trick. I was finishing my time and excited about the prospect of travelling for a while. I drank and partied and caused havoc.

I had been on guard one Saturday, so Carl, an English legionnaire, and I went to town for breakfast on Sunday. Carl told me about his recent trip to Sarajevo with the Fourth Company. He had left the building one day and been shot through the arm by a sniper. Three weeks later as he left the hospital he hadn't even arrived at the bottom of the steps before he was shot through the hand and returned straight back to hospital. The commanding officer wouldn't let him out after that, believing three times unlucky. Carl died a year later at the age of 23. I don't know how he died but I guess it was coming. Sometimes people are just unlucky.

We started breakfast with steak and chips and a beer. One beer led to another, which led to BMWs, and by the afternoon we were stinking drunk. Later that evening we went to Emile's and fell asleep on the bar. We had forgotten to put in our leave passes so eventually we were picked up by the military police and taken back to camp. I staggered in to the captain's office and tried to keep my balance as I saluted, but I just staggered from side to side. I slurred a half-hearted presentation before looking back for Carl who was in a far worse state than me. He couldn't walk so he crawled up the office steps and halfway through the door before trying to salute, but as he lifted his arm he slumped to the ground. I couldn't help but laugh.

'En taule! En taule!' We were dragged to a prison cell to sleep it off. The next day we presented to the captain in our parade uniforms and received seven days' imprisonment. Each day we rose at 4.30 am to sweep the camp and do menial tasks. We weren't beaten or beasted as we knew the *garde de la taule*, who was my old friend Stein from the 1st Company, and I was now a senior corporal. In the evenings at around ten o'clock, 20 of us would cram into a small dark room with our sleeping bags and find a place on the floor. I stood on Carl's shoulders when I heard the familiar whisper of Ray who was outside with a case of beer. The small barred window allowed enough room for me to put my hand through and drop the ball of string, being careful to keep hold of one end. I pulled up the case of beer and pulled it to the window ledge. One by one I passed the beers down to the lads. Before sleeping, I put them back in the case. First thing in the morning I would jump up to the roof and hide the evidence. Life in this prison wasn't too bad now.

One evening I decided to go to the bar near the sergeant's mess before getting a taxi to town. I had known the bar was there but I had never been inside. It was a strange place. I wondered if it was a brothel. A few girls lived there but I wasn't sure if they were prostitutes. I chatted to a Corsican girl in her early thirties. She had the dark features and hair typical of the southern Mediterranean. Her teeth were slightly dark also. I bought her a couple of beers and thought, 'what the hell!', and invited her out to town with me for a drink. We called a taxi and I took her to the 'Bar Select'. A few of the lads were already drinking so I bought the Corsican girl a beer. We propped up the bar for an hour before she suddenly changed. She had held her purse close to her all night continuously looking inside. I grinned at the lads as she pointed the pistol in my face before waving it around the bar. 'This girl's nuts,' I thought. The small-calibre tol had a silver body and a wooden handle, fitting nicely in her bag. It was too small to be a 9 millimetre – I thought it was probably a 2.2.

'Personne vas me baiser et me quitter … comprenez? … personne ferait ca encore!' 'No one's going to fuck me and leave me … understand? … No one will do that again!'

I thought, 'Yes, you are probably right!' I looked down the barrel. 'There is no way I'm going anywhere near you!' I left her in the bar and went to 'Chez Emile'. Annabel was still there. She was a nice girl. Emile had left for a while. He was too ill from his sickness.

I had met Ray again. He was still in the First Company and Le Loup was cracking codes for his money. They were both corporals too. We all went out to the foyer for a beer. A young English lad had arrived. He reminded me of myself when I arrived. He was a little older but he still sported the once baby faced features that I had lost through the sun and many a fight. I called him *gironne* (babyface) and he grinned, obviously very familiar with the term. I commented on how young he looked and Le Loup replied:

'Oooouui, mais tu vois sa gueule dans cinq ans, tu ne lui reconnais pas.' 'Yeah, but you see his head in five years, you won't even recognize him.'

Le Loup was right. This was a factory that turned lads into men, chefs into killers, policemen into hooligans, officers into private soldiers, the untrusting into the trusting, and it was a system that worked if you stayed long enough for it to happen. But I did not regret staying; I was proud of it. We legionnaires had a bond that only those that had served would understand. Inside the Legion walls we were all brothers – we had all become a part of a unique family.

Ray and I decided to rent a two-bedroomed apartment in town. It was a beautiful place with two large rooms and a balcony overlooking the town and the bay. On Saturday afternoons we would sit and chat. One of the local barmaids would always come around. She was besotted with Ray and yet I never saw him with any girls during the five years. We would sit on the balcony looking at the beautiful mountains shadowing the bay while we drank Kronenbourg. It was nice to live like this. Every spare evening I was in town or at 'home' and my life was my own. I had done my time and now I was left alone. The Legion became quite a normal way of life for a while. So many people desert and never really get to see the other side of how life could be. They usually return to put it down in order to save face. If I had stayed

I would no longer have to wear my uniform in town; I could get married; I would get my corporal-chef stripe in a couple of years, so I would not need to attend roll-call; I could have a bank account and in some regiments even have a car. If you had done your minimum contract then you were respected for becoming a legionnaire and your life was given back to you. It just took a little stamina and tolerance.

Mac came to visit in the early spring. He had finished his contract a few months earlier after his two-year tour of Djibouti. We had planned to travel around the world in a 4x4, something we didn't really succeed in doing. He had considered staying in the Legion as had I, but we had both made commitments to each other to travel so we left. He was in Calvi for a month in which we went into town at every opportunity drinking BMWs and looking for girls. I had met a girl in the 'Son des Guitares' a few times but I wasn't very forthcoming. Eventually, late one evening she asked me:

'Ça te dérange si je dors avec toi ce soir?' 'Does it bother you if I sleep with you tonight?'

I hadn't had sex since leave a few months previously, but acted as if this happened to me on a daily basis.

'Uuuuuuhhhh ... d'accord.'

'Uuuuuuuuhhhhh ...' Effective reflective pause ... 'ok then.' Secretly, I thanked the gods before I returned to her flat, which was in the same block as mine. She made love to me while snorting cocaine but it felt no different to me!

Mac and I got into the habit of climbing the cranes, which were on the building sites to the rear of the bars. After a dozen bottles of Heineken and a dozen more

BMWs, as the sun was beginning to rise over the mountains, we set about the task of getting to the end of the jib before doing a few pull-ups. I had no fear of heights or death. It was totally natural in my youthful state of mind to climb around without regard to safety. Jean-Louis, the owner of the bar, would tell us about a time when he worked on the scaffolds and a friend of his fell to his death while mucking about. We assured him in our drunken states that all was fine and not to worry.

I was coming to the end of my five years. In a last-ditched attempt to get me to stay the clerk was told to write 're-engaged for six months' on my identity card. I was aware of the trick and many men had just thought what the hell, and stayed.

I was thinking of what I should do next. I sat on my balcony early that morning, watching the sun rise and thought about the things I had seen. The people I had met and how I had become like them. I had drunk, swore and slept with prostitutes. I had seen a different side of life and I had friends that I would die for. I had turned from an innocent baby-faced boy into a man, and I looked at the world through different, harder, deeper eyes. I was content in my aggression and hate. It fuelled me. It made me strong. The Legion had done its job and made me a legionnaire for life. I considered staying. I would have if I had not promised Mac who had already left that I would travel with him for a while. I put on a bit of REM and thought again for the first time in years. I could feel the alcohol in my fingers and it felt good. I was chilled out to the bone. I was happy and looking forward to the rest of my life.

*

The day before I left the 2eme REP I had a leaving party in the company bar. Many other lads arrived from the other companies. The captain gave me a plaque with my name and the time I had served the company. It matched the one the colonel had given me during the day with the certificate stating that I had served in the Legion for five years. I had collected a few plaques and badges from my various postings with different units in the Legion. They would all be kept in a box in a cupboard at home for few years or, when I was married, in the toilet; the only place besides the shed that most husbands are allowed to have as their own! I looked around at the men in the room and the pictures on the wall. I'd had a long hard five years and it was soon to end. I was sad to leave my friends and yet glad to start the next chapter of my life. Eventually, the crowds dispersed and we met up in town. It was now the early hours. Ray and I were packed ready to return to Aubagne to hand in our kit.

The following morning I watched the Corsican mountains disappear from the stern of the ferry. In Aubagne the colonel asked me once more if I would like to stay for a career but I refused. I never was much of a career man: I just joined for the experience; to enjoy the good bits and forget the bad. I slept in my clothes to avoid catching *morbacks* (crabs) from the bedding for a final time. From behind me I heard Grant's familiar chirpy voice with its soft southern Irish drawl.

'The last time I saw you, you shook my hand and said, "See you in five years," and here we are!' It was great to see him. He had spent the first two years in French

Guyana with the 3rd Foreign Legion Infantry Regiment (3 REI) before going to the 2 REI in Nimes. Belge was also there, having spent his five years with the REP. I didn't see anyone else from when I joined. I wondered if they had decided to stay or deserted. I asked Grant, who told me most of the men with him had deserted and a couple had died of overdoses of cocaine in South America, where it was as cheap as chips. I was nostalgic to see Grant after five years and know that we had both made it through to the end. We went around the various offices to finish our paperwork. In the *Bureau des Anciens de la Légion Etrangère* (BALE, the former legionnaires' bureau) an adjutant told me that I had earned a small pension when retirement age came: he gave me a card, which stated that I was a former legionnaire and that if I was ever in trouble to present it to the nearest French consulate and they would help me. I looked at the green card, which entitled me to residency in France, and I read the unemployment forms that would allow me to claim benefits in France if I wished. I didn't use these documents but I still retain them just in case.

We paraded in front of the Monument aux Morts, which was a huge white memorial for the Legion dead. It had been dismantled and brought back to France from Sidi Bel Abbes, when the Legion left Algeria in the early sixties after more than a hundred years of war. About 15 of us stood in a line in our civilian clothes and I wondered where the forty blokes I had finished basic training with had gone. Of the 15 standing, only a handful had joined up with me – the rest were either retiring or leaving after signing further contracts. I presented to the general for the last time. He shook my hand and looked me in the eyes:

'I hope you find what you are looking for in life. Are you coming back?'

'No, mon général.'

'A gauche gauche!' We turned to the left and marched away to our bags. I walked through the same black iron gates, turned and saluted, before walking back to the railway station, passing the garages where I had slept rough the night before I joined.

A Poem

When the shadows are long
There is a time to sit and think
Think of the places I've been
And the people I've seen.

When the shadows are long
And it's late at night
I talk to the God in my head
Who never sleeps.

I tell him the thoughts of the day
That are not mine.

When the shadows are long
And you have time to read these lines
Think of it not as a poem
But a song to the tunes of my mind.

Tony Sloane

······ EPILOGUE

It would take a few years before my Legion training and indoctrination would return me to any kind of 'normality'. For a couple of years I would sleep with my fists clenched and wake up if anybody walked into the room, jumping up in the en-garde position ready to fight the intruder. It would take a few more years to stop drinking during the week and save it for once or twice at the weekends.

I joined the French Foreign Legion as a naive young boy. Partly with a sense of adventure, but it was more the result of a turbulent and disrupted childhood. I am not proud of some of the things I did while serving; reflecting upon the person that I was it seems hard to imagine this was me. Although ashamed of some of these incidents I don't regret them either – each one is a thread in the tapestry of my life. I am forever proud to have served with the Legion and become a legionnaire. It gave me a veritable understanding of trust and respect, which will stay with me for the rest of my life.

I would not like readers to walk away with the impression that the Legion is a totally brutal and unwelcoming place. Each man that joins has a different experience. It may be that my time with the particular people I served alongside seems rather harsh: however, others may have had a far different five years. I chose to join the famed 2eme REP and volunteered for a two-year stint in Africa, whereas others who joined with me chose to play an instrument in the Legion band, write articles for the *Képi Blanc* magazine or work in an office, and thus enjoyed a slightly more relaxed existence. The Legion is not teeming with brutality – only a small part of it harbours a much-outdated regime.

Upon leaving I briefly travelled around Europe and America with Mac. Once my savings were exhausted I joined the British Parachute Regiment. I was, as the Legion would say, 'inept for civilian life'. Towards my early thirties I realized, through yoga, meditation and studying philosophy, that enough was enough and it was time to move on to something different, the allure of operations and combat losing its appeal. For the moment I now work as a private security consultant.

I would like to dedicate this book to grieving widows and fatherless children of fallen soldiers.

GLOSSARY

appel roll-call (6 am and 10 pm) (French)

bakshish small amount of money, as in a charge for services rendered (Arabic)

beasting rough treatment used as punishment

bonhomme a partner, buddy (French)

bordel slang, whorehouse or disarray; also exclamation (French)

casse-croûte snack, break-time (French)

équipement webbing or harness, containing the magazines and kit (French)

espèce d'enculé slang, 'arsefucker'; also exclamation (French)

Famas 5.56-calibre assault rifle made for French army in St-Etienne

groupe de combat rifle section of 8 to 10 men (French)

gueule slang, dog face, usually used as aggressive insult (French)

jerrycan flat-sided metal container of liquids

live range area for shooting with live ammunition

merde slang, shit, exclamation (French)

muzzle flash flash of fire from the end of gun barrel/muzzle

niah prostitute (local dialect)

ops military operations

promotion training course (French)

putain/pute slang, whore; also slang exclamation (French)

sac à dos rucksack (normally a Bergan) (French)

Section de Combat 30- to 40-man rifle platoon

stagging on mounting the guard (also on-stag)

taule military prison (French)

tracer bullet or shell made visible by trail of flames or smoke

VLRA Light Reconnaissance Vehicle

wadi dry riverbed

Zodiac inflatable rubber assault boat

Zone de Saut Drop Zone

.... APPENDIX

Structure of the 2eme REP

The 2eme REP consists of seven companies.

• One Compagnie de Commandement et des services (CCS) – Headquarters and Service Company.

Function: Supports the chef du corp (regiment commanding officer, full colonel) by running the regiment services and maintaining the camp when the regiment is away.

• One Compagnie d'Eclairage et d'Appuis (CEA) – Support Company.

Function: Comprises two Sections (Platoons) of Milan anti-tank, one Section of 20-millimetre anti-aircraft guns, one Section of 81-millimetre and 120-millimetre mortar and a Reconnaissance Section working from Jeeps.

• Four Compagnies de Combat – Rifle Companies: known as the 1st (Première), 2nd (Deuxième), 3rd (Troisième) and 4th (Quatrième) Compagnies de Combat. Each of which consists of four Sections (Platoons) of approximately forty to forty-six men, divided into four Groupes de Combat (Rifle Sections) of ten or more legionnaires.

• First Company. (Tony Sloane's company.)
Function: performs anti-tank roles, night fighting, urban operations and specializes in combating snipers.

• Second Company. Function: specializes in arctic and mountain warfare, overcoming obstacles and clearance problems.

• Third Company. Function: specializes in amphibious operations.

• Fourth Company. Function: specializes in clandestine operations including explosives, demolition and sniping.

• One Groupe de Commandos Parachutistes, formally known as Les C.R.A.P. (Les Commandos de Recherche et d'Action en Profondeur, or Forward Reconnaissance Commandos).

Function: These are the elite of the French Foreign Legion, who specialize in all aspects of combat training including HALO parachuting (High Altitude Low Opening parachuting, where oxygen is required to facilitate the jump).